Our Debt to Greece and Rome

EDITORS
GEORGE DEPUE HADZSITS, PH.D.

DAVID MOORE ROBINSON, PH.D., LL.D.

STOICISM
AND ITS INFLUENCE

BY
R. M. WENLEY
PROFESSOR OF PHILOSOPHY

COOPER SQUARE PUBLISHERS, INC.
NEW YORK
1963

Published 1963 by Cooper Square Publishers, Inc.
59 Fourth Avenue, New York 3, N. Y.
Library of Congress Catalog Card No. 63-10288

PRINTED IN THE UNITED STATES OF AMERICA

PREFACE

HISTORIANS, even historians of philosophy, have tended to dismiss Stoicism lightly, and popular opinion has taken the cue. No doubt, relevant reasons abound. The riches of Socrates, Democritus, Plato, and Aristotle served to accentuate the comparative poverty of the next age. Its effort over, Hellenic genius was no longer capable of following the argument whithersoever it led. Serene, fearless treatment of fundamental problems gave place to subjective musings, which ran to whim sometimes. Sanity and balance gone, extravagant or, eventually, fantastic theories found audience. The barbarians — so the Attic Greek would have reckoned them — had their revenge when ‘ asianism ’ waxed, raising irrelevant issues. Above all, pregnant social changes displaced the centre of interest. Nevertheless, it was a far cry (more than five centuries intervene) from the earliest to the latest Stoics and, thanks precisely to social changes, philosophy did acquire

fresh significance. Hence, although a protest rather than a science, an outgrowth of
emotional stress rather than of intellectual
curiosity, Stoicism was destined to rank among
the formative ethico-political movements characteristic of the western world. Despite its
obvious shortcomings, despite its lack of originality, circumstances lent it an influence
destined to survive for generations.

Recognizing this, recent investigators have
laid new stress on the movement, viewing it
as typical of a recurrent attitude toward the
tragic mystery of life. Moreover, seeing that
we no longer account philosophy a web of
curious speculation, but one among the several
most symptomatic expressions of human activity, we may anticipate that similar situations
will produce similar ideas. For, transitions
make strange bedfellows. Accordingly, Stoicism may well turn out congenial or, at least,
suggestive, from time to time. ' Neo-Stoicism '
enlists votaries today. This little book is
conceived in some such spirit. The aim of
this *Series*, and stringent limitations of space,
dictate its scope. It must deal, not with the
technique of a system, but with a type of
generalization so persistent as to have become

a factor in the idea, ' Humanity.' Hence, it were prudent to confront peculiar difficulties forthwith.

Of course, all generalizations are subtle, evasive, dangerous; a slight change in emphasis may well transform perspective. This goes without saying. Nor do I need to insist that, among hundreds of Stoics, known or nameless, we possess intimate acquaintance with very few. Full sources fail us. Here again, it goes without saying that, seeing we lack eighty per cent of Euripides, the most popular ancient dramatist, it were futile to indulge anticipation about aloof thinkers, critical reformers, and house chaplains.

On the other hand, the peculiar difficulties are inseparable from the great gulf fixed between the Hellenic and any post-Christian outlook. I select three by way of admonition; a fourth, because it sheds a ray of hope. (1) Hellenic ' society ' had a background of its own, a complex of use and wont, hard to realize now. Conventions, manners, moral judgments, institutions, politics, in short, all the vital processes of common life, developed associations so characteristic that language itself tends to baffle transfer. For instance, try to find an English equivalent for *kalo-kagathos*. Select the word 'gentleman,' then note how current esteems and disesteems mock comprehension of the Greek. Age-old positive prejudgments operate in such a case.[1] But negatives are no less important. (2) Recall, then, that although pioneers of the scientific temper, the Greeks would have been left quite cold by our phrase, " the scientific view of the universe." Indeed, our 'universe' had no existence for them. Let alone their innocence of inductive causality, the hesitations of their soberest intellect, Aristotle, about the precise meaning of ' Nature ' (*Phusis*) may suffice to give pause. Occult interferences, presumed resemblances and dualities, were normal events with them. (3) Myth saturated their religion, so much so that a select spirit like Plato seized this form, sometimes, truth to tell, the substance. The curious tale at the close of the *Gorgias* may be taken in illustration, merely because it is less difficult to grasp than many others! Nay, the Greeks loved solutions or ironical sophistications on this wise where we detect intractable problems. With them, as with all men, religion embodied an effort to adjust *their* world-order to emo-

tional demands. Whatever the permanent
kinship in emotion, world-orders differ for
confusion. Accordingly, to point the moral,
we must resist manifold temptations to read
our ideas into Greek culture; above all, perhaps, we must eschew spiritual reactions
evoked by the word ' God.' True, *Theos,* like
God, implied a supernal power, but a power
over against men, not One touched in all
things like as we are.

Nevertheless, stress the contrasts as we
please, there is a continuity. For (4), the
Greeks could not keep their ' society,' ' science,'
and ' religion ' in watertight compartments as
the manner of some is now. A ceaseless in-
terpenetration set their approach, with one
startling consequence worth note. In these
days, the specialist was unknown. Had he
shown himself, he would have been dismissed
promptly as a fit companion for slaves.[2] The
Greek mind, clear in its simplicity, dealt freely,
naturally, unconsciously, with life as a whole:
the modern mind, lost in mazes of detail, is
being forced back upon the same ultimate con-
frontation. Moreover, following the great
tradition, the Stoics worked with material
drawn almost at random from ' society,'

'science,' and 'religion,' material mirroring perdurable questions in politics and government, metaphysics and science, religion and theology, character and conduct. In this respect at least, they continue to throb with our pulsations.

CONTENTS

[xi]

STOICISM
AND ITS INFLUENCE

STOICISM AND ITS INFLUENCE

I. INTRODUCTORY

THE tendency to minimize, misunderstand, or even forget the Stoic movement, has, and always must have, one obvious reason. The 'golden age' of Greece in the fifth and fourth centuries B.C. owes its splendour to the attraction exerted by Athens upon foreign ability, and to her unparalleled fecundity in native genius. A full score of eminent men compel mention, of whom a large proportion rank among the foremost, not merely of their own, but of all time. *Æschylus*, *Polygnotus*, Anaxagoras, *Phidias*, Protagoras, Gorgias, Herodotus, Prodicus, *Sophocles*, *Euripides*, *Thucydides*, *Pericles*, *Antiphon*, Zeuxis, Hippias, *Socrates*, *Aristophanes*, and *Xenophon* belong to the great epoch, between 460 and 400 B.C. Despite the disastrous Peloponnesian war, the inspiration 'of this period could not pass; prompted by it, Lysias, *Isocrates*, *Praxiteles*, *Plato*, *Demosthenes*, and Aristotle — the two philosophers conspicuously — caught and set forth its essential spirit. They flourished between 380 and 325 B.C. It was impossible to escape the glamour of such a galaxy.[3] More than a century after the death of Socrates, the Macedonian king, Demetrius Poliocertes, could fervently call Athens "the beacon-tower of the world." She remained its spiritual centre. For, although originative power had gone two generations ere the sack by Sulla (86 B.C.), the illustrious dead for whom he spared the living, as he said, ruled from their urns. So, despite the mean reputation of contemporary Athenians, lowest in the days of Tiberius (25 A.D.), the endowments of Marcus Aurelius (176 A.D.) evidenced vital faith in the historic city till, at length, the confiscation of Justinian (529 A.D.) ended a continuous tradition of nigh one thousand years. While, later, with Christianity thinking in terms of Greek philosophy, with Aristotle "the master of those who know" since Dante, and with Plato as the medium between educated men since the Renaissance, the magic of the *Geniezeit* never failed. Accordingly, to adjust the balance, some imagination is requisite, some traffic with hard facts.

The heyday of the Athenian state may be put in 451 B.C., when the Law was enacted requiring proof of Athenian parentage on both sides for citizenship. Keen sense of mighty, almost superhuman achievement, and of high privilege, bred consciousness of intense mutuality. The city would become a close corporation.[4] But clouds streaked the horizon already.

It stands to reason that the tiny Greek states attained their unique position because they were able to demand, the citizens willing to give, public service nigh beyond our comprehension. The separation or opposition between the State and the individual, one of the most powerful motives in contemporary politics and thought, would have passed the ken of Cato and Cicero, to say nothing of Pericles and Plato. It was not that Athens — some others even more — suppressed personal activity or 'private life.' On the contrary, the citizen never conceived 'freedom' as absence of restraint; it was the privilege of personal participation in every public affair. " Liberty of action " implied instant obedience arising from familiar consent to a set of values saturating the group. Hence, despite the in-

tolerable claims of the community as we should
judge them, the Greek cities proved fertile in
conspicuous individuals. They produced men
of like mind, of Hellenic sympathy, of ability
to hold large conceptions with pellucid insight.
Agreement about the kind of humanity worth
fine attachment bred truest freedom out of
apparent subordination. The great Greeks
saved their lives by losing them. Their energy
and self-sacrifice had for reward a perfection
reached by no other historical people. Free-
will creatures of their own culture, they became
creators and architects of the humane spirit
in all ages everywhere.

Pericles' Funeral Oration [5] epitomized this
stage. It fell from a spacious soul elevated by
wistful memories and stirring hope. A transcript from life, it was no capricious invention
or ' occasional piece.' Of course, poltroons and
shirkers, braggarts and rascals could be found.
But the general conscience, annealed between
Marathon and Salamis, asserted gracious sway.
Thus it was that the great Greeks " walked
in light." Yet, they were neither children nor
gods. And so

" *The yawning wants and gnawing cares of life* "

[6]

could not but return for judgment. Ill-fated warfare between ' the Good ' and ' goods ' broke forth as always.[6] Economic opportunity (spiritual and educational no less than material) attracted numerous alien immigrants; economic pressure pandered to immediate advantage; superficial prosperity loosed a mood of recklessness and this, in turn, gave rise to the domineering selfishness that wrecked generous coöperation. Moral tone slackening, irresponsibility led to faction; while the keen stimulus of traffic with enlarged affairs made debate inevitable.[7] Hence, within a generation after Salamis, " the men of the fathers " found themselves under fire and, long ere calamitous Ægospotami (405 B.C.), " the gifts of the gods and the resolutions of wise men " were beset by hostile criticism, often at the instigation of aliens. Not without resentment, native and therefore able to strike back by political means: witness the attacks upon Anaxagoras and Aspasia, the public humiliation of Pericles himself, the charges against Diagoras, the derogatory tales about Protagoras and Prodicus, the emigration of Euripides and, as a culmination, the martyrdom of Socrates; notice the predominance of alien names. All to no purpose. In the long run, disillusion was to have its way with the citizenry, political defeat going hand in hand with dissolvent thought. 'Tainting' outlanders aside, the Greeks, grown restless and shifty, were afloat on a sea of inconvenient problems. What is the State? What is the justification for its paternal guidance of the citizen? What is Law? What is Concord? What is Justice? What is Liberty? Do the gods merit worship? Ere long, the very foundations of common confidence were subjected to ironical scrutiny, the bare possibility of Knowledge or Truth was scouted on street-corners. Plato and Aristotle left no successors. Their grave insistence on the self-forgetfulness of duty gave place to the doctrine that the only good government renders government superfluous, that liberty is gained at a stroke by dispensation from every sort of obedience. For the rest, " the resources of civilization " are enlisted in a gigantic conspiracy to enslave the human spirit. Therefore it is necessary to renounce the State, in order that each man apart may possess his own life. " The ideal of harmony which we carry about in our bosoms " appeals to infinite

sanctions by comparison with the decent con-
formities of the estimable citizen. Recognizing this, the ' wise man ' will go his own way,
to realize his true freedom as a ' citizen of the
world.' Stoicism arose toward the ebb of this
welter, when the Greek was on the point of
performing a new function in a transformed
political order. Yet, although he had drifted
far from the old moorings, he could neither
forget nor forego the achievements of his
people. His fresh privilege it was to assess
them and readjust them for the guidance of
mankind.

II. THE STORY OF STOICISM

IMAGINATION is necessary, not merely to appreciate Greece of the great age, but, perhaps more important, to escape it! Modern parallels may lend stimulus. The death of Pericles is separated from the organization of the Stoa [8] by about one hundred and thirty-five years. The same period precisely intervenes between the Massachusetts insurrection, with the subsequent call of the Convention to draft a Federal Constitution or, to take a European event, between the Assembly of Notables, and the present day. Now, all Europeans (and some Americans) may be forgiven if they ask, What was the Massachusetts insurrection? All Americans, Lafayette's membership despite, (and most Europeans) may be forgiven if they ask, What was the Assembly of Notables? So completely have these matters, once crucial, fled the field of contemporary interest. It may be affirmed that the transformation of the ancient world over an identical period was even more subversive. The United States and France remain, self-governing groups: Greece had gone, never to regain autonomy. For, consider what had happened: Athenian hegemony ruined by the destruction of one fleet at Syracuse, the surrender of another at Ægospotami; the collapse of victorious Sparta before the Thebans at Leuctra (371 B.C.); resultant embitterment of antipathies between and within the Greek cities, which made foreign aggression easy; the subjection of Greece to Macedon by the defeat at Chæronea (338 B.C.); the sensational career (more extraordinary in its consequences, probably, than in itself) of Alexander, who founded Alexandria (destined to contest the intellectual supremacy of Athens), and set up a colossal realm; the dissolution of this personal dominion on his death (323 B.C.), and the hectic rise of similar monarchies amid bewildering turns of fortune, fraught with decisive influence upon the future of Greece; finally, the contact of Rome with the Hellenic peninsula, thanks to the adventures of Pyrrhus (280 B.C.), the first vague hint to the Roman Senate that it must subdue the entire Mediterranean area. In a sentence, the Hellenic political unit, the independent city, had seen its day; henceforth it was to be absorbed in motley empires which, mingling Asia with the west, blurred the sharp distinction between Greek and ' barbarian.' These tremendous events had settled in their courses, deflecting the old order, ere Stoicism appeared and, as always, thought found its point of departure in life. The Greek youth of 290 B.C. was scarcely less remote from Platonic higher politics than the American lad now is from the scrupulous prelections of his countrymen who followed Reid and Hamilton.

Were one able to recapture the outlook of primitive man, it might be possible to agree with Plato, that philosophy is the child of wonder. But, once reflection has had its way, philosophy usually arises from contradiction; difficulties slurred and, as a rule, unforeseen antitheses, excite comment or doubt. New knowledge, too, and changing social conditions are active factors. Still, continuity holds, because contradiction presupposes something that has been or has come about. Now, Hellenic thought developed in ' schools,' not primarily in our use of this term, however. The word *schole* meant leisure, ease; hence, next, 'a work of leisure' — a discussion by those who have enjoyed the *slow* opportunity to master ideas; only at last, and with a kind of degradation, a place where such chaffer prevails or, worse, where men traffic in the things of the mind. A Greek 'school,' then, was an association of select souls; under the leadership of a mentor freely chosen, they tried, not indeed to escape the passing show, but to attain deeper insight. They were dealing with spiritual things spiritually discerned, learning that the universe of values holds the clue to the universe of objects. Their aim was the enrichment of personality, in the sense that, to be a person, a "man must have raised all mere instincts to the level of intelligence." In particular, they clung to the conviction that personality is ethical, exists as a 'relation of thought' — a state of mind, if you will. Here was an avocation, slow, if sure. Plato spent we do not know how many years with Cratylus, Socrates, and Euclid; Aristotle's association with Plato covered the last twenty years of the great master's life; Zeno was in contact with Crates, Stilpo, Polemo, Xenocrates and Diodorus for many years before he felt himself able to make an independent start. But the doctrine of a ' school ' readily crystallizes into convention. It grows a mannerism simple to acquire, or even a reputable pastime (*diagoge*). A mature product of a civilization, it may be transferred, and parroted without much trouble. If so, it cannot penetrate the person. Consequently, a fresh survey of the world and self must ensue, if individual emotion and original ideas are to contribute their due. The antitheses, say, between the mystical and the rational in Plato, between final and efficient causes in Aristotle, but chiefly between the mental habits of past and present Athens, rendered some survey of the kind inevitable. For, while the leaders who succeeded Plato and Aristotle — the Aristotelians notably — were men of character or vast learning, creative impulse had waned, amazing vicissitudes having overset the situation.

Under these circumstances, aliens, nay, Greek-speaking strangers, were heirs to a double advantage. On the one hand, they had not been subjected to the subtle pressure of Athenian tradition, on the other, they intervened with a new background, and so saw with open eye. Accordingly, it is worth note that, of thirteen Stoics reputed associates of Zeno, not one was a native of Athens, while, perhaps more significant, seven came from regions where the migrant Semite had settled for centuries. Moreover, such was the strength of the foreign element that seven heads of the Stoic sect (five from the Semitic fringe) had come and gone ere native Athenians gained the leadership; by this time, one hundred and eighty-three years having elapsed, Stoicism had lost its early thrust. Zeno, the founder, was no Attic gentleman, but the son of a Phœnician merchant of Citium, in Cyprus, who visited Athens in the course of business, bringing the youth with him. We are not aware what tendencies marked the culture of such folk; nevertheless, they must have been quite ' un-Athenian.' Surviving gossip about Zeno intimates as much.

We have just seen that the Greek was a man of ideas; the Semite was anything but this, and a touch of Greek education (which Zeno probably had) could not suppress his nature. The Athenian thought in terms of a past friendly to humane achievement, although at some points the beauty of the world, consciousness of high mission, and warrantable pride in gracious success, could not conceal sorely inexplicable mischances. The Semite thought in terms of a future which, laying an imperative 'ought' upon him, led him to believe that he must conquer by his own action, even when others hindered or were cold. He would abrogate prescriptions if they raised obstacles to his independent rule of self. He never enrolled as " one of the golden youths of Ephesus who has spent his whole life in contemplating, admiring, and worshipping the wonderful temple of the goddess." On the contrary, he would forthtell — " in our inner life also there is a universe . . . no more dost thou number, no more dost thou meas-ure, for every step is in the infinite." Be this as it may, when Zeno arrived at Athens and took stock of the various 'schools,' he found his first kin among the Cynics, who had been preaching — and practising — just such doc-trine for a generation. Crates looked the very man for him. But brilliant irrespon-sibility, crude surliness, and plebeian wit proved vacuous on closer acquaintance, al-though the rigour of self-denial left a deep mark on Zeno. So, in search of real knowl-edge, he betook himself to other 'schools,' to the Megarians, the Old Academy, and the eclectics of the day. Eventually, gathering his own circle in the Porch, he launched a new movement, with valuable countenance from that much misrepresented patriot Antig-onus Gonatas, the Macedonian king (319–239 B.C.).[9]

During Zeno's life, his group prospered, attracting not a few able disciples. His immediate successor, Cleanthes (head of the ' school ' 264–232 B.C.), despite a certain stolid industry, failed to maintain comfortable ascendancy, and secessions occurred, possibly because Zenonian doctrine, drawn from many sources, had not come by unity. Indeed, Cleanthes himself seems to have been more critical than originative. The system was to be smoothly rounded by Chrysippus, according to all accounts a great figure, the third head of the ' school ' (232–206 B.C.). He gave much attention to logic, clarified and hardened Stoic materialism and, thanks to mastery of the dialectic and ' word-chopping ' so dear to the clever Greek, fathered many of the paradoxes distinctive of the sect, tooth-some to its enemies. The first or constructive stage of Stoicism may be said to close with his

strenuous, honourable, and widely influential
career.

A dozen names or so and some meagre
hints survive from the period between the
death of Chrysippus and the Embassy of
Philosophers to Rome (155 B.C.). Zeno of
Tarsus led the Porch (208–180 B.C.), to be
succeeded by Diogenes of Seleucia (180–152
B.C.), he by another Tarsian, Antipater (152–
128 B.C.). Zeno may have held unorthodox
(Platonic) views about physics; Diogenes
shone as a dialectician and, more significant,
may have written a book on Divination;
while, as significant of another drift, Antipater may have reverted to Cynic severity.
Fortunately, abundant evidence avails to
illuminate the political whirligig — " a king
today, and tomorrow he shall die (*Ecclesias-
ticus*, x. 10). Over the broad area of
Alexander's empire, " the robbers of thy
people shall exalt themselves to establish the
vision; but they shall fail " (*Daniel*, xi. 14).
However, these vicissitudes affected the
Macedonian *condottieri* and their merce-
naries; the general march of civilization sped
its own way. Above the clash of battle, certain mental and moral tendencies persisted.

Hellenistic culture crystallized, with fateful issues for Stoicism, and Alexandria, its chief centre, was bidding against Athens for intellectual supremacy, indeed Eratosthenes (*c.* 276–196 B.C.) had already given her prestige and the lead she was to follow.

Alexander the Great founded many new, transformed many old towns in Syria and Egypt. This was no capricious whim. These cities followed the Hellenic model, because the Greek state had come to set the type by its magistral success. Moreover, the upper classes, then as always representatives of the preferable standard of life, approved Hellenic culture and customs. " They built a place of exercise [gymnasium] in Jerusalem according to the laws of the Gentiles (*I Maccabees*, i. 14); and caused the noblest of the young men to wear the [Greek] cap " (*II Maccabees*, iv. 12). If this was possible in the Holy City of the Jews, it is easy to see how far hellenization might go when welcome or met by no stern opposition. Indeed, Strabo's (the Stoic geographer, *c.* 29 B.C.) eulogy of Tarsus in his time may be taken as one consummation of a general movement. " Such an enthusiasm for philosophy and all the other branches of a liberal education has been fostered in the people of this city that they have outdone Athens, and Alexandria, and all other places one might mention as seats of learning and philosophical study." The consequences — they included Christianity — were epoch-making. Hellenic culture, emigrating to teach the earth, lost its clear serenity, thanks to absorption of oriental traits. Besides, when reproduced by Syrians, Phrygians, and the rest of the " multitude " mentioned by St. Paul (*Acts*, ii. 9–11), the wanton Levantine temperament left a trail. At Athens itself strange gods acquired naturalization; Magna Mater, and her shameless orgies, had gained a footing in the days of Chrysippus. Briefly, the rational interpretation of man and the world, the glory of Greek thought, found a theosophic rival, invested with the subtile mystery of the immemorial East. Private associations — confessedly on the plan of the old Hellenic *Thiasotae*, which had lent form to the philosophical schools — multiplied everywhere, to propagate the new cults. Greek ideas saturated the ' barbarian,' but paid the price in debasement by Asiatic superstition. Spiritual unrest seethed, scepticism grew fashionable, and the dogmatic schools, Stoicism most prominent, took the defensive perforce.

Contact with the Roman directing class (155 B.C.) may be said to mark the transition from the Old to the Middle Stoa which, in turn, gave place to another development after Cicero's murder (43 B.C.). Two men of power, encyclopædic learning, and remarkable influence, overshadowed their contemporaries: Panætius of Rhodes (*c.* 189–109 B.C.) and his pupil, Posidonius of Apamea in Syria, (135–51 B.C.), Cicero's master. The 'great world' of the day rather than the quiet 'school' claimed them. Their careers attest the new era more than their doctrines.

Stoicism as a system received its final shape from Chrysippus. An amalgam, it proved ductile under pressure of personal, philosophical, social, and religious forces. To begin with, Attic Greece held most definite ideas about the dignity of intellectual work. Other pursuits were vulgar (*banausikos*) or, as we say now, illiberal. Plato's acerbity toward the Sophists is traceable more to his

disgust with their ' bad form ' than with their
views. But, recollect, this attitude presupposed the standards of Periclean society. It
was shameful to permit money-changers in
the temple of thought, to traffic in the things
of the mind. At the same time, Attic thinkers — Plato himself, and Aristotle — stood
ready to advise ' tyrants,' kings, and other
rulers. Chrysippus preserved this tradition
in his friendship with Antigonus Gonatas,
though not with the old inflexibility to the
proprieties. Acceptance of fees, or even
patronage by the prosperous, no longer
brought loss of caste. He admits " three ways
of earning an honest livelihood — teaching,
courting the rich, serving states and princes."
It is true that Hellenic prohibitions died hard;
we find them in Panætius and, much later,
in Diogenes Laërtius (*c.* 200 A.D.), who says:
" Life resembles a spectacle. Some attend it
to participate in the contests; others to do
business; the best, to look on. So it is in
life: the vulgar seek fame or money; the philosophers, truth." Nevertheless, Panætius
himself witnessing, the philosopher *did* find
wider opportunities outside the classroom, as
we may call it. He ranked as a public charac-

ter, an expert sought by the powerful as well
as by the youth; he put a stiff price on his
services, got a good living, amassed wealth
sometimes.

Naturally, the audience and the occasion
affected style and substance alike. The manner veered toward rhetoric, while the 'practical,' so-called, loomed big. Thus, making
a profound obeisance to the principles of a
system, he proceeded to deal with less strenuous subjects, more accessible to the mind of
the many. Detail intruded, temporary affairs
came under review, hortatory discourses were
in request. There can be little doubt that
these tendencies prevailed after 150 B.C.,
sinking eventually to the level of the pompous
convention or impudent charlatanism flogged
by Juvenal (c. 90 A.D.), and Lucian (c. 170
A.D.). Hence, it is fair to class Panætius and
Posidonius as pliant Stoics. The one may have
protested against occultism in the real spirit of
the system; in the same spirit, the other may
have devoted himself to meteorology, mathematics, and geography. It remains true that
both were deft to vary stress, mindful of concession, apt in rearrangement. Eclecticism had
marked them for its own. Panætius examined

[23]

cases of conduct, not disdaining casuistry, in his capacity of missionary to the Roman oligarchy, whom speculation bored. Nor could he keep himself from the dangerous quicksands of spiritism, a strong religious drift compelling. Posidonius' five books "About Prognostication" must have diverged far from Stoic materialism; they certainly gybed with the time, lending him the vogue which "contributed most to the final acceptance of sidereal divination" (astrology): this, again, was to affect "the development of the entire Roman theology more than anything else." [10] In short, with both, the fundamental principles of the system receded before matters pertinent to moral precept, hortatory edification, or reinforcement of faith. Eloquence with geniality, a reversion to conspicuous Platonic traits, served Panætius and *his* Stoicism well. Courageous inquiry, savouring of Aristotle although accommodated to contemporary pietism by more than a tincture of the *Timæus*, made Posidonius the most noteworthy intellectual of the day. But, precisely the temper of both punctuated a lapse from systematic principle, and presaged greater changes soon to come. The exuberant curiosity, scientific zest, and objective balance of the Hellenic mind had become a tale that is told. Not for three and a half centuries were they to flash for the last time in Plotinus.

On the other hand, Stoicism reaped great compensations. Fading as a four-square theory, it grasped power as a moral influence. A small scale analogy may serve to drive the point home. No nation has been more thoroughly imbued with Protestant Christianity than the Scotch; their character literally bristles with it, from the dour bluntness of the literate peasant to the protective loquacious irony of Thomas Carlyle. Remove it, and you render the national spirit inconceivable. Yet, to the best of my knowledge, Scotland has not bred a single theologian of the first rank. Similarly with Stoicism. Not a single thinker of the first rank appears, but the temper

> " *Far back, through creeks and inlets making,*
> *Comes silent, flooding in, the main.*"

After the destruction of Carthage (146 B.C.), it rapidly insinuated itself into the very fabric of Mediterranean culture. At length, thanks to the plunderings of Cicero, the broad dis-

[25]

cipleship of Virgil (*c.* 23 B.C.) and Philo (*c.* 40 A.D.), the left-handed propaganda of Plutarch (*c.* 100 A.D.), and the affinities of the New Testament (*c.* 56–120 A.D.); to the 'natural Christianity' of Seneca (*c.* 60 A.D.), the rugged sincerity of Epictetus (*c.* 116 A.D.), and the stark pathos of Marcus Aurelius Antoninus (*c.* 176 A.D.), it sank deep into the "thousands of silent moments between the striking hours" of human destiny. For, consider, it is one of the five formative heritages bequeathed to western civilization by the ancient world. The others are Hellenic delicacy of perception and poise of thought, the organization of the Roman Empire, the normative principles of Roman law, and Christianity! No one can tell how far the modern order has taken mould from Stoicism any more than he can tell what it owes to Greece, Rome, or the spirit of Christianity — all are so subtly ubiquitous.

The antagonistic judgments, to say nothing of the acrimonious disputes, converging upon Cicero, prove him a pivotal figure. His qualities and defects do not concern us here; his unique importance admits no denial. The fact is, he stood at the cross-roads. Although he disliked Stoicism for years, fate made him the bridge between the Middle and Later (or Roman) Stoa. The inward temper at the time is difficult to penetrate, nay, its shades of thought and feeling still baffle us in many respects. Be this as it may, two movements, running athwart one another, puzzled the 'practical' Roman, and Stoicism was destined to mediate.

Roman political sagacity — Marcus Porcius Cato (*c.* 184 B.C.) its memorable exponent — stressed the necessity to walk in the old paths. Later Greek thought dallied with a type of selfhood withdrawn from political relations. Leanings of this sort are already evident in Scipio Africanus the Younger and his circle (*c.* 140 B.C.). The resultant struggle between the ideals of the compact group and of the footloose individual offer one clue to the spiritual drama of the decline and fall of the republican oligarchy, in which Cicero played an ingenuous part — *quem bonum civem semper habuisset, bonum virum pateretur.*

The Romans were a strong breed and, this very strength sustaining, felt *free* to accept ancient traditions, to bow before august in-

[27]

stitutions, to ascribe the expansive power of
their city to supernatural guidance rather than
to their own efforts, and to rest satisfied with
the stolid virtues that lent tenacity to Roman
character, stability to civil law, majestic urge
to Roman policy. The moral fibre of their
victorious Republic struck them as the chief-
est of "the long results of time." Quite
lacking the speculative insight of the Greek,
worldly achievement appealed to them, and
they were content, even gratified, to bethink
them of the solid virility, the instinctive
obedience, which had won so much. Hence,
one popular conviction, surprising enough to
us, was perfectly natural. As the Roman
reasoned, the best officials would spring from
families — whether patrician like the Cornelii
and Claudii, or plebeian like the Licinii and
Marii — who had developed a sense of responsibility in the service of the state. In the
long run, such men came to be esteemed
Senate 'material' — and the Senate was
Rome: the three hundred from "every most
excellent citizen of any rank," scrutinized by
the Censors. And 'excellence' — how determine it? Obviously, by open record in the
conduct of public affairs. Thus, former oc-

cupants of the great offices, successful soldiers, and sons of eminent citizens *were* ' excellent.' Consequently, in a state nominally democratic, an inner oligarchy, based on social superiority and political distinction, controlled the initiative or legislative as well as the executive functions of government. On the whole, till the Social War (90 B.C.), the mass of the citizens were content to have it so. It must be insisted, then, that the authority of the Senate was a moral power, emanating from a profound realization of mutuality.

Moribus antiquis res stat Romana virisque.

These words of Ennius, which Cicero likened to an oracle, — a species of divine revelation, — cannot be translated literally. They are surcharged with the temper that rendered senatorial rule not merely possible but grateful. They give us an inkling why the people heard the Senate gladly. The poet seeks to affirm that everything which bestows guarantee of permanence upon Roman greatness roots in unbroken operation and authority of ethical qualities and that, as the generations pass, these qualities must be kept alive in the persons of strong, dutiful men. Transfer our word ' devout ' from the religious to the socio-political sphere, and you may catch the implication. In short, Ennius appeals to the grave persuasions born of settled conscience. They have proven their inestimable worth in the past — *circumspice;* they can be maintained in the future only by the fortitude and consistency of the citizens. Endure for them, and you *have* welfare, because you enjoy righteousness in and through the commonwealth, whence alone any personal possession of value can be derived. The Attic Greek, democratic minded, would discharge this duty himself. The Roman, oligarchic minded, delegated its discharge in the large things to those whom he deemed fit, because they and their forebears had been faithful time out of mind. He caught his own express image and person in the moral authority of the Senate, an assembly of kings, acting for a sovereign people. Now, this is to say that a type of character, " something of the centurion," presented itself perdurable. As Virgil has it: Indwelling, a spirit sustains, and one mind pervading every member impels the entire group, and blends with the noble reality.

But should the Senate evidence betrayal of

this virtue, what of individuals? Will not the ties of mutuality between the citizen and his state slacken, and this without *stasis* or faction, as the Greeks called it, but with a novel claim on the part of the separate soul? This claim, central to Stoic doctrine, asserted itself after the Hellenic cities lost independence, and put a new aspect upon the appropriate qualities of a meritorious life. Notwithstanding, the character-type just described still stood forth an exemplar, indefeasible from folk-memory. When the 'wise man' of the Stoic came to inspire the dubious citizen, the individual had been discovered, asking, To what profit is *my* life? Cicero is elusive,

> " *Wandering between two worlds, one dead,*
> *The other powerless to be born.*"

Roman public activity the breath of his nostrils, he had ample ground for his suspicion of Stoicism; but, especially toward the pitiful end, the Stoic ideal always returned at once abashing and cleansing.

One is tempted to say that Cicero pursued all the philosophies, particularly the easiest, but running off on a half-truth confounds confusion. The great advocate merely displayed

the constitutional timidity of the Roman mind
and, perhaps, the effect of his profession. As
he avers, philosophy was a real interest from
the first, not an after-thought, nor yet a body
of rhetorical exercises. Still, urgent business
engrossing, he seems to have parried ultimate
problems, only to find himself stricken by
them at length. In any case, he is not to be
judged harshly, intellectual conditions being
what they were. There is reason to believe
that, of the three spokesmen who formed the
Greek Embassy to Rome, Carneades, the
Academic, was the ablest, certainly he mo-
nopolized public attention — the others were
Critolaus, the Peripatetic, and Diogenes of
Seleucia, the Stoic. Now, after the death of
Chrysippus, Carneades touched the prevalent
disorder with his scepticism to such purpose
that general acceptance of Stoicism was hindered till the religious revival made headway
and, when the scale did turn, profounder
issues had been abandoned in favour of a
philosophy " intended to show what is chiefly
necessary for a happy life."

Cicero always accounted himself an Academic. While it is true that he softened the
denials of Carneades, habit led him to look

on both sides of a case, to judge probability
the safer guide, to despair of universal solutions as beyond reach; " accuse nature, who
has completely hid truth in an abyss." The
needs of the advocate and practical politician
told their tale here, rejecting Stoic dogmatism.
But, after all, few minds can rest in possibili-
ties, and manifest tendencies of the day were
bound to reduce these few to a vanishing
point. Moreover, Polybius (*c.* 207–122 B.C.)
had given currency to the notion of an ' education of the human race.' " Fortune has
swayed almost all the affairs in the world to
one centre [Rome], and compelled every force
to set in one and the same direction." In
addition, he had detected the presence of an
Overruling Power in the success of the Romans, Greek though he was. " I think that
the Roman state is held together by a quality
which is a reproach among other men — I
mean scrupulous respect for the gods. For
this motive is heightened in effect and enters
into the public life of the people and into
public affairs to an almost incredible extent. . . . Whenever it is difficult or impossible for human power to apprehend causes,
we may fairly in our uncertainty refer such

things to divine interposition or Fortune."
Even so, he could not eliminate human co-
operation. " Where it is possible to discover
the originating and efficient cause of what has
occurred, in such cases I think it wrong to
refer it to the will of heaven." Cicero felt all
this acutely, his circle seemed for a brilliant
moment to be bearers of the Genius of Rome.
" Be to yourself the Senate; wherever the
manifest destiny of the commonwealth leads,
follow." He also felt — however some of his
actions may have belied him — that individuals must live as under the eye of a great
Taskmaster [11] — Cato the Younger an overwhelming proof, and reproof. So, despite the
theory of probability imbibed from teachers
in youth, he clung to some divine Source of
order, and emphasized the indispensable rôle
played by good citizens as its vicegerent.
" There is nothing which divine Power cannot
accomplish." " Law has not been devised by
human ingenuity, nor by simple legislative
decree, but is an eternal principle which must
direct the whole universe, enjoining and forbidding everything with wisdom." But man
has his part. " There is no life, whether in
public or private affairs, whether at home or

abroad, whether personal or in association
with others, void of obligation. In the due
discharge of this consists all the honour of
life, in its neglect the odiousness." "Know
therefore that thou art a spiritual being, since
it is a divine Power within thee which moves
. . . and governs . . . exactly as the sovereign
deity governs the world." Theology of a kind,
and the ideal of moral tenacity became his
sheet-anchors. Thus, at long and last, the
temper of Stoicism rather than Academic
subtlety unveiled " the nature of what is."
Recall, too, that this " nature " was no private affair, a mere parenthesis in the life of a
citizen, but the inflexible sense of public responsibility which backed the divine Fortune
of the Commonwealth with the sleepless
vigilance of submission. In a word, Cicero's
interpretation of the Greek mind to Roman
character rendered it inevitable that the
future should belong to the sainted Cato, heir
of Socrates and Diogenes, that is, to the good
(or ' wise ') man leagued with the Power behind events.

I have lingered with Cicero because I
believe him to have mediated a decisive transition.[12] His philosophy may be altogether de-

rivative, for this very reason it gains significance as a symptom. Setting great store on Greek culture (Book V of *De Finibus* happily survives to tell), he naturalized it in a larger world, launching it on a career of unforeseen influence much more religious than philosophical in mood, thanks to power of seizing and adapting other elements. The Stoicism familiar to the average man of the Christian west, the Stoicism which, percolating into our civilization, must be reckoned with still, — the Stoicism of Seneca, Epictetus, and Marcus Aurelius, — owes its course to a combination of forces. Posidonius and Cicero were the dominant personal factors. So much so, that the words spoken by him of Cato are Cicero's best epitaph: *Etiam mortui valuit auctoritas*. But, ere the consummation in Roman Stoicism, other influences intervened.

In this connection, it is suggestive that Cicero's most powerful work — most ominous for its author too — was the Second Philippic, the most perfect, *De Oratore:* a formal oration and a treatise on public speech. After 160 B.C., when the 'grammarian' Crates of Mallus, son of Timocrates the Stoic, visited and taught at Rome, higher literary instruction

[36]

made its way slowly in face of opposition, as
the decrees of the Senate (161 B.C.) and of
the Censors (92 B.C.) show. By the later years
of the Republic it had become necessary " both
as a means of defence and of acquiring reputation." Indeed, Roman youths who, like Julius
Cæsar and Cicero, anticipated an official career,
went abroad to complete their training, Athens
being still their chief ' university town.' Power
of speech marked the royal road to influence,
nay, it was an indispensable qualification for
the Roman directing class; the remarks of
Tacitus on the oratory of the Emperors give
proof.[13] As a consequence, the subject-matter of education underwent change, and humane culture based on Greek models acquired
preëminence. Naturally, philosophy formed
a staple along with poetry, but philosophy as
an introduction to the give-and-take of life
rather than as a ' science ' for its own sake.
It was the handmaid of Rhetoric. Moreover, the transformation of opportunity attendant upon the passage from Republic
to Empire accentuated inbred temptations
toward trifling. Effects that Tacitus could no
more than hint Dio Cassius was at liberty
to make plain. The events that happened

after the assumption of supreme power by Augustus could not be related as those that preceded. " Before that period everything, even though it happened far from Rome, was brought before the Senate and the people, and was therefore known to all and recorded by many. . . . After this period public affairs began for the most part to be transacted secretly and by means that were not divulged." Free speech gone and, with it, civic responsibility, even able men betook themselves to elegant trifling, a badge of their class; while serious spirits, driven from a larger world, were fain to map the infinitesimal parish of their private souls, a sure, if devious, way round to morose piety or egotistic platitude. The silence of Roman philosophy, Quintus Sextius aside, in the seventy-five years between the death of Varro and Seneca's return from exile (49 A.D.) betokens much. And, when the silence broke, the Later Stoa was to reveal a temper all its own. For, another movement had done its subtle work. Weary, men were seeking some object worthy their allegiance, and had turned to religion, with diverse results.

The ' religious reaction,' so called, in the

Mediterranean area during the two centuries before and the three centuries after the appearance of Christianity, is so complex, adequate knowledge so recent, that no attempt can be made to grapple with it here. However, a general notion of the movement is essential seeing that Roman Stoicism was part and parcel of the medley.

We are reminded by Schopenhauer that religion is the only metaphysics which the people can ever understand. In other words, a religious stir and a philosophical school differ by breadth of appeal. Now, within the Roman dominions there was, as always, wide divergence between sections of the folk, over and above differences peculiar to race. Three *strata* are discernible: the masses, urban and rural; a cultivated class cast in the mould of a specific education for specific ends; and a very few who might be termed specialists, though not at all in the modern sense. The ' religious reaction ' could not but affect these groups variously.

We have reason to believe that the directing class, the inhabitants of Rome, and the people of the Provinces in more immediate contact with the metropolis, sensed a void; nor was it merely that the ghastly anarchy of the Social and Civil Wars, the doubtful, long-drawn issues of the Ciceronian age ending in the domestic and foreign turmoil of the years between Julius Cæsar's death and the Principate of Octavius Augustus, had left indelible marks. For, even amid the benefits of peace within and without conferred by the prince who was verily "God come back," a nameless unease, amounting to fear sometimes, assailed men.

In externals, a new Jerusalem might have descended out of heaven; it could not assuage spiritual yearning, the outgrowth of moral poverty. Accordingly, the most suggestive of Roman poets hymned the new empire, but the while, his heart, close to the universal heart, beat to the rhythm of a profound sadness. "A mist of unshed tears seems to haunt the stream of Virgil's genius." The great poet served himself the representative of a great tradition and yet, being a "white soul" warm with revealing love, his piety shuddered before the manifest decay of Roman character and, thus shaken, he left a half-unwilling confession,

"Majestic in its sadness at the doubtful doom of human kind."

The void could not be evaded and, eager to fill it, men went their several ways, unanimous only in a vague conviction that some cure must be forthcoming. Unaware of their part in the greatest transition of history, they did not detect that the successive subjugations of Egypt, Spain, Cappadocia, and Judæa marked the beginning of an end: by 180 A.D., the 'classical' spirit had fled forever. Nor can we blame them, seeing that conscious judgment, full-throated and final, was reserved for Jerome (*c.* 390 A.D.): *Romanus orbis ruit.* The more then is it necessary for our comprehension of Later Stoicism to stress the lapse of the old temper.

There can be little doubt that prolonged contact with alien civilizations gradually altered the Roman outlook. The Punic wars marked a stage and, thereafter, the old Family and State gods lost influence, particularly in the cities, conspicuously in Rome itself. On the other hand, the sobriety of the original civic religion, bemused by luxury and shaken by scepticism, gave place to mystic yearning. In any case, the ancient simplicities failed to satisfy, and their essentials fell into discard. Complication of life and, in all likelihood, the call of this world, developed abnormal situations with an appeal to occult powers. Doctrines of 'double truth' commended themselves even to the reflective. Thus, whatever the more or less naïve nature of the early Roman deities may have been, there was a general reversion to animism ("the world is full of spirits" akin to man) among the urban population. Unknown, vague beings, capable of evil and, sometimes, of good, were to be swayed or conciliated in order that their power might operate for human welfare here and hereafter. Magical rites, traditional or recent, multiplied on every hand, to exert persuasion. In short, materialism, the characteristic accompaniment of superstition, marked the 'worship' of ancient minor and novel major deities, furnishing the means whereby their caprice might be offset, their interest enlisted. The old State religion had become an affair of parade for the directing classes who, otherwise, were beginning to seek gods able to guarantee personal salvation,

[42]

and to find them in the private oriental cults.
Nevertheless, the scientific temper of Greek
thought, even in its Hellenistic guise, detected
an ' order in the universe,' indifferent to men,
it was true, but capable of being turned to
their advantage were it but understood. Hence
Divination, with an abundant crop of dreams,
forebodings, portents, and predictions, came
into vogue and was accredited widely by the
pontifical approbation of authoritative persons like Posidonius and Nigidius Figulus
(*c*. 60 B.C.). The half-contemptuous, half-
cynical attitude of Carneades and, more symptomatic, the " rage and sorrow " of Lucretius,
attest vivid recognition of the dangers inseparable from these tendencies, and from the less
disreputable magic of astrology. But protest
availed nothing, because the emotionalism of
thaumaturgy and animism, the pretensions of
a sacerdotal caste, and the universal practice of ' consulting the stars,' filled the place
left vacant by the death of the old oracles,
adjusting themselves to contemporary unrest.
Even Tacitus could recount the miracles of
Vespasian with complete gravity; while such
terms as ' jovial,' ' martial,' ' mercurial,'
' saturnine,' and ' lunatic ' survive to illustrate

[43]

widespread conviction of the 'sympathy' of the heavenly orbs with human fortune. Thus, two currents intermingled: a more or less honest spirituality, founded on recognition of the majesty of the order of the universe, leading insensibly toward a naturalistic monotheism; and a tangle of superstition, ranging from crudest wizardry to forecast of sacrament.

In these circumstances, 'specialists,' the Stoics foremost, found themselves confronted with a clamant problem and an overwhelming public opinion. Their doctrine of Fate was unfavorable to personal religion, because it made gods of all shades equally with men subjects of an inviolable order. Accordingly, they adopted Divination, and its main instrument, astrology, as a possible means of investigation. Some issues of Fate might be laid bare, at all events the opportunity to learn was worth trial. To this extent they drifted with a stream of tendency easier to follow than to fight. But they were troubled by practical questions especially oppressive in Rome itself. Daily life had developed peculiar reasons for uncertainty. Neither Princes nor Senators knew their mutual posi-

tion and precise authority. As a result, each
suspected the other, and resentment waxed
ominously. Scions of the old governing families abominated the freedmen of the imperial
household, but the spread of delation, with its
glittering rewards, placed them at a terrible
disadvantage. The new senatorial families,
commonly alien to Italy, aspired to be more
' Roman ' than the Romans, but were at a loss
to know what exactly ' Roman ' involved.
With all, plain ideals and necessary compro-
mises grew more and more at open odds.
Worthy ends seemed unattainable thanks to
low means; on the contrary, vulgar and de-
spicable means, to their very despite, might
ensure partial realization of the best ends.
Hence a new moral psychology, almost though
not quite casuistical, came to be supplied by
the Stoics. The practical demand proved so
urgent that the principles of the system fell
into the background, and the effort to furnish
a ' guide of life ' became synonymous with
' philosophy.' Counsels of perfection, and
personal examination, designed to relieve
stress, or to steel men impotent in face of an
amoral tyranny and a world-order charged
with eventual doom, clouded free intellect and,

as is usual under such strain, the 'spiritual director' ran the possible gamut. Beset by frailty, he might be a contemptible sycophant or selfish charlatan; persuaded by noble resolve or high insight, he might be the sole witness to that energy of faith whereby life here below is delivered from blank despair, — the betrayal of Thrasea was a shrewd thrust at virtue itself!

The so-called 'Stoic' opposition to the Cæsars, and Seneca (*fl.* 33–65 A.D.) emerge from this welter. The one, difficult to appraise because partly political, partly social, partly moral, sheds illuminating side-lights upon dark features of the period. The other, difficult to appreciate fairly, embodies the total effect of the interplay of many forces upon a pliable character who, while achieving a career in accord with the aspirations of his family, strove to safeguard duty despite most untoward circumstances.

Any attempt to evoke the imponderables of long ago is dubious and, as a rule, one must suspect his own judgment save in the large. Thus, it is more or less obvious that opposition to the rule of one man found voice a generation before the Principate. Cicero

was a tragic figure because his ideals bore
small relation to contemporary political necessities. His fluent imagination harked
back to Rome as the ancient city-state reborn
more glorious, to the Senate as the heir and
guardian of Athenian ' democratic ' principles.
He sensed neither the actual facts nor the impending problems. Supremacy attained, with
Rome now the universal umpire, a personal
bond to link communities of most varied cul-
tures had become indispensable. In the same
way, a competent civil service capable of ad-
ministering the multitudinous details of government, and of guaranteeing something like equal
justice from day to day between all who were
bound to look to Rome for guidance and
safety, grew fortuitously when not organized
specially. Small wonder, then, that Cicero's
widespread vogue set the *city* in unfortunate
perspective, and rendered the Senate jealous
of outworn privileges at the very moment when
it might have been prompt to adjust itself to
urgent responsibilities. No new worlds remained to conquer, but a very new world
clamoured for readjustment. Accordingly,
two myths arose together — a myth about the
Roman Senate, and a myth about Julius

Cæsar, easily transferred to his successors. Senatorial legitimacy, Cato its representative saint, had dropped out of practical politics, to flourish as *the* 'republican' ideal. This was the first myth. On the other hand, a man holding purely human responsibilities, careful of the concerns of others, firm in danger, and not fearful of contracting unpopularity in defence of the public welfare, a man at once submissive to the law and prepared to enforce it without scruple, was the last recourse in the nature of the case. So Tiberius said, thinking no doubt in terms set down later by Gaius: " There are hardly any other men who have such power over their sons as we." And this lonely soul, pitiful in power, who gravely laid his dearest private relations on the altar of public duty — a veritable incarnation of Roman quality and defect — was abundantly right. Yet, thanks to the second myth (of a purely self-seeking tyranny), he rang down the corridors of history as a bestial tyrant.

Like all myths, these held a kernel of truth. The Senate, a legislative and executive body from time immemorial, found itself reduced to the level of a consultative council under the Empire. Moreover, even this influential func-

tion suffered from the competition of the
Equestrian Order, which was gradually ab-
sorbing finance and recruiting the incipient
civil service. Then, too, the Order swarmed
with men whom the senatorial party counted
inferiors — a mob of freedmen, Egyptians,
Levantines, and even Jews — " they that are
of Cæsar's household " (*Philippians*, iv. 22).
Besides, promotion to lucrative offices had
ceased to be an exclusive perquisite of the
Senate, and many members felt real or fancied
slights. In short, political and social developments conspired increasingly to drive
senatorial circles into opposition. Certainly,
they formed a natural centre of permanent
discontent or ready disaffection. As to the
Emperor himself — the inhabitants of Rome
proved but human. Set on a pinnacle without
precedent, he drew all eyes, served the target
for every sort of comment, apposite or base-
less. Flying rumours and obscene jests of
the streets; free gossip of fashionable or, worse,
would-be fashionable, cliques; careless small
talk at vapid, if luxurious, entertainments;
irresponsible, suggestive ditties; the idealiza-
tion into dirt of ' best sellers '; lampoons, the
more witty the more indecent; patter of the

comic stage converged upon prominent folk
in imperial Rome as in every capital, from the
Athens of Pericles to the Paris of Gambetta
and the Washington of Woodrow Wilson; it
must be insisted, too, that conduct at which we
would stand aghast ranked normal under the
best princes. Hence, thanks to the fragmental
truth behind the myths, the metropolis formed
a seedplot of unrest, alleged ' republican.'

Of such were the lower levels, where ignorance, turpitude, envy, selfishness, pique and
the baser passions spawned aggravation. Augustus knew what he was about — as usual —
when he applied the *Lex Majestatis* to libel,
or to heedless utterance concerning the head of
the State, as well as to sheer treason, or to
pusillanimity in face of a foe, the practice of
the Republic. Profession despite, Stoics had
been caught in this gallery. But a higher
mood, reverting to the honour, self-mastery,
tenacity, or even legalism of the old directing
families, could still prevail, the ancient prestige
of the Senate, preserved imaginatively from
generation to generation, assisting powerfully.
This bred the true ' Stoic opposition,' sometimes to the eternal credit of the School, at
others with the *doctrinaire* fanaticism that

[50]

always exasperates. For, when the *Lex Majestatis* became an instrument of tyranny, or a tool of base cupidity, upright men stood in need of principles and of consolation; character was the sole possession that could not be filched from them. Even so, signs multiply that Stoicism is fast hardening into a mood, an attitude toward life. For, the ' opposition ' took many forms by no means ' Stoic ' exclusively. Literary, political, social, moral and cultural manifestations may be detected; moreover, these appear in a variety of combinations, so that the philosophical factor, dominating as it sometimes is, can seldom lay claim to sole influence. The literary expression serves to illustrate this.

Persius and Lucan, Tacitus and Juvenal two generations later, intimate an atmosphere, in spite of their emphatic personal equations. Youth though he still was at death, Persius embodied a distinct cultural savour — Stoicism with a conception of the chief good: " O ye souls that cleave to earth and have nothing heavenly in you! how can it answer to introduce the spirit of the age into the temple-service, and infer what the gods like from this sinful pampered flesh of ours? " —

countering the philistinism favoured by contemporary social changes. Lucan, his scepticism notwithstanding (perhaps a trait of youth), feels that dire circumstance is too strong for character, loss of political liberty having set the wicked in high places. Accordingly, his disgust drifts perilously nigh the morbid, a clear defect of Roman Stoicism in certain aspects. Tacitus, thoroughly alive to what might be morbid or unreasonable in the Stoicism of the recent past, yet speaks for the 'party of virtue,' and reverts with a curious sardonic wistfulness to the 'good old times,' finding content much more in grim declamation than in sober inquiry; a strange pose for a historian. Juvenal, like Tacitus haunted by the memories of a seventy years' nightmare, excoriates vice, the forcing-ground of every evil. Contrast them with Livy, and you find that both despair of those moral qualities which had ballasted Roman political talent and, to this extent, evince Stoic pessimism in face of monitory decline. They *felt* rather than knew consciously that, when a Nero could be the most popular of princes on account of lavishness with " bread and games," the metropolitan mob was ready to barter free

citizenship for a mess of pottage. Thus, startling as were the contrasts between the possible
outlook of subjects of the Claudians and
Domitian on the one hand, of Vespasian,
Nerva and Trajan on the other, a common
mood, essentially Stoic, rises to the eye.

The political opposition, motivated chiefly
by the Catonian legend (now a faith of high
degree), presents something of a puzzle. On
the whole, the Empire had been accepted; at
least it had no practicable competitor. Pætus
and Arria, Annæus Cornutus, Musonius Rufus,
Thrasea and the younger Arria, Afranius
Burrus, Arulenus Rusticus, Herennius Senecio
and Junius Mauricus, Helvidius and Fannia,
foremost among many prophets, apostles and
martyrs of militant Stoicism, diverge according
to their several lights. Yet, agreeing in austerity, they embodied a moral no less than a
political impulse, the one operating positively,
the other negatively. Idealizing the mighty
days of the republican oligarchy, some of them
looked askance at the Empire, but their proud
disdain and contemptuous aversion were reserved for the vicious emperors and the dis-
graceful minions of the imperial household.
When the political factor held the upper hand,

as with Pætus and Helvidius, a visionary intransigeance, glorious yet impossible, marked them for its own. Honourable protestants against facile corruption and enervating toadyism, they were relics of moral dignity — too much mere relics possibly. Hardness made them half-saints; lacking the seraphic gleam, if not brow-beaters, they failed to persuade. Untouched by beatitude, they struck not a few of their contemporaries as unreasonable or obtuse, and straitened by the bonds of a thin, perhaps unlovely spirit. Nevertheless, faced with dreadful odds, they ' felt the noblest ' and, suffering the insomnia of morality, they left behind

> " A *voice that in the distance far away*
> W*akens the slumbering ages.*"

Their political activity futile, they yet sealed the moral temper of Stoicism, so that it passed on to Western civilization, to reproduce coercive values never lost since. Tactless, they bore most rigorously upon themselves; arid, they witnessed an unshaken faith; hoping against hope, they gave their all, even life itself, for the conservation of ideals. Not in vain. For, softened by a later mood, their spirit came to sit on the imperial throne and, accentuating the puritan strain in Christianity, proved its inherent worth by the onset of a power able to persuade to this day. The life *is* more than raiment! But, what life? The life that sweetens the world, being charged with a vision of the communion of the saints? The life that turns away from earth and its vanities, with a surly or feeble confession of futility? Or, the life fascinated with life, although keenly aware that the manifestation of the sons of God must be postponed for a season, thanks to the frailty of creatures handicapped by blind mischance, confusion of values, disease, and the brevity of time? Or, again, the life that distills consolatory vocation from its share with every man in an inclusive ethical kingdom, where devotion to the loftiest purposes transmutes the ills of fleshly helplessness? It is at once the secret and the puzzle of Seneca that the extremes of Christian conviction of victory and pagan sense of defeat were alike impossible for him. His it was to give Stoic moralism its final bent, but in the medium of a culture belonging wholly to this world. " The man with any historical imagination must be struck with

STOICISM AND ITS INFLUENCE

amazement that such spiritual detachment, such lofty moral ideals, so pure an enthusiasm for the salvation of souls, should emerge from a palace reeking with all the crimes of the haunted races of Greek legend." [14]

We often forget that the importance of an unusual person may be indicated by criticism as well as by praise, to say nothing of discipleship. Judged by this test, Seneca stands high. Indeed, he effaced Cicero at times, and he has awakened endless curiosity.[15] In truth, he had a dual importance. On the one hand, he was the most representative figure of Roman civilization in his day, " the leader in letters and the leader in government," as Pliny the Elder testifies. His very prominence proved his undoing, nay, undid him for posterity in a measure. The question recurred continually — Was Seneca a saint or a *poseur*, " always ours," as Christian Fathers boasted, or the weak-kneed hypocrite of Macaulayan bunkum? [16] Now, this is to say that he possessed a secret and so, for a fair estimate, account must be taken of his opportunities and temptations, of his traditions and education, of his aspirations and expedients.

He belonged to the second generation of

Spanish provincial immigrants, a notable group who adopted Rome enthusiastically. It would be misleading to dub him a ' climber.' But the very success of his father, who reached the Equestrian Order, rendered an official career the cynosure of the family. Accordingly, his brothers, Gallio, whom St. Paul has immortalized, and Mela, who, though better known for his son, the poet Lucan, gained influential position and comfortable fortune, were typical. Seneca was to surpass them. He won unique success and, in the issue, bore the heavier burdens. Strive as he might, he could not be altogether himself; indeed, he urges repeatedly the virtue of conformity. His dubious health — he seems to have been of those who are never ill and never well — did not help him. Moreover, thanks no doubt to a cautious father, he underwent a thorough education of the kind then approved as *the* preparation for public life. Warned against philosophy by this circumspect parent, as if it were the mark of devotion to some cranky cult, he turned to the rhetoric of the day. His style shouts this at us. Here too, he enjoyed the advantage, felt the restraints, of tradition. From the time of Bion of Borysthenis (*fl.* 250 B.C.), the Minor Socratics, the Cyrenaics and Cynics especially, had decked philosophy in wit and epigram. Menippian satire, which Seneca is supposed to have imitated in that famous-infamous *jeu d'esprit, The Pumpkinification of Claudius,* furnished a possible link in the transmisson of this habit. At all events, the style was *sententiosum et argutum,* as Cicero objects, — ' sententious ' in the sense of paradoxical, antithetic, tricked with phrases easily separable from the context, and thus apt to pass into common talk. Seneca had the stock maxims of philosophical ' diatribe ' and, likely enough, the ascetic bent, from Sotion of Alexandria and Papirius Fabianus, his Sextian and Stoic mentors; from the rhetors, the mannerisms and methods of oratorical ' declamation '; from all, backed by the politico-legal career and the intellectual conventions of the age, the pragmatic pose, — *vitae, non scholae discimus.* " Mental triangles are pointed, but their points won't wound." These traits appear in his colloquialisms, in his effort to " clothe and adorn the obscurity even of philosophy itself with sensible and plausible elocution," to drive thought home by ingenious touches. Hence his ' urbanity,'

cleverly sly; hence, too, his zeal to beat the
gold thin, and Quintilian's regret that Seneca,
"in speaking his own mind, had not the
advantage of control by the *taste* of another."
Thus, he suffered from the very qualities of
his education and, withal, allowance must be
made for a period when artifice simulated art.
The same ought to be said of his political and
social entanglements even if, puzzling as they
must have been, they helped him to grasp
the real issues of life in maturity.

But, every inimical circumstance notwithstanding, one must insist that Seneca brought
an original talent to the difficult situation.
He excels even Tacitus in thrust of *individu-
alizing* moral analysis. The brevity and
powerlessness of human life, dark death its
final end and sole certainty, yet craven despair impossible, and the liberty of truth to
self alone worth endeavour, are crystal
clear; he will not abate any by a jot.
Rather, tracking them through, as they harry
or enhearten the common man, he tries to
hint how the tragedy may be borne. Increase
of knowledge and, be it remembered, increase
of experience too, serve to sharpen the issue,
not only in "that hard Pagan world," but

always. So much he sees to be in the nature of the case. Thus beset, otiose " felicity is an unquiet thing . . . some heads bear it better than others, but it dissolves all." Consequently, no matter what the time or place, one resource remains, attainable by him who has learned to govern character:

> " Strengthen the wavering line,
> Stablish, continue our march,
> On, to the bound of the waste,
> On, to the City of God."

Freed from epigrammatic moralizings, and from a doctrine of indifference that seems to justify any compromise, this message rings out, essential. Need we wonder that, nerved by its haughty spirit, men have reverted to *this* Stoicism ever and anon, deeming increase of knowledge and experience mere accidents by contrast? Indeed, such has been the power of the appeal that some feel constrained to deplore its sway over certain types of Christianity.

Although Tacitus treats him with curbed respect, there are signs that Seneca went out of fashion under the Flavian emperors (70–

96 A.D.). Later, Epictetus and Marcus
Aurelius never mention him. The reasons
must be sought in a subtle change of imponderables. To begin with, his doctrine
was bound to arouse opposition in circles
where baseness or sensuality reaped specious
reward. Its " imitation of the old Romans "
(' republicans '), its frigid tolerance of
worldly aims, its stress upon personal independence, — upon " arrogant indolence " de-
tractors said, — its self-consciousness perilously nigh vanity, irritated when they did not
abash. " Openly inimical to the prince's
[Nero] amusements," reputable and disreputable alike, Seneca became the object of
" stealthy calumnies," as Tacitus records.
Nor was this all; these were but the more obvious sequels. Parodoxically enough, his connection with a court sordid beyond belief, his
consequent wealth suspected of taint, his ac-
commodations as a man of the ' great world,'
(in the case of Agrippina, for example), not
to mention his ' airs and graces,' were little to
the liking of the next generation sobered
somewhat by Flavian reforms. His very
kindliness served to suggest cowardice or, at
best, pliability. Dangerous though it may

have been to teach virtue in the Golden House, even this hazard could not suffice ignorant masses bethinking themselves of salvation of the soul. We are far removed from Cicero's "assuredly the Cynic plan of life is to be rejected, for it is incompatible with modest reserve," and from his lukewarm attitude to religion, — a palliative, not a gospel. Musonius Rufus, Helvidius Priscus, Epictetus, and perhaps Demonax, witness a rebirth of Cynicism; they depart even further than Seneca from theoretic Stoicism, to emphasize beneficence, forgiveness, above all, single truth to self. The oldest Stoicism, the Stoicism aflame with fresh ardour, is about to become the second last word of the movement. On the other hand, Plutarch, Dio Chrysostom, and Maximus of Tyre, represent that effort to calm human fear in face of the intolerable mystery of life which, appealing to emotion by way of immemorial sentiment, made Senecan and Stoic intellectualism at once insufficient and archaic. For, whatever can be said of Seneca otherwise, he was *not* at home in the universe. The Cynic development claims our attention here.

Whatever the spectacular excesses of some

early Cynics (*c.* 380–300 B.C.), the intent of
the sect is plain. They laboured ' in travail,'
and sought ' deliverance ' from the gyves of
civic life, believing themselves faithful to the
Socratic ' inner light.' They would be set
apart as the " organ of imperial Reason." And
if at this time, as in the latest phase under
the Roman empire, they warranted much foul
scandal, proving by the maxim, " all is vanity,"
that the greatest of vanities may well be the
preacher himself, they yet expressed a mood of
profound alienation, which the ancient world
never shook off. When a Chrysippus could
renounce political activity with, " If I counsel
honourably, I shall offend the citizens, if
basely, the gods," he had no recourse but to
ask, " What can *I* be to Zeus? " If a Seneca
were so blind to the significance of the advent
of empire as to dismiss it with a contemptuous phrase,— " the freebooting outrages of
Alexander," — what remained but to seek the
divine, *within* the remotest depths of his own
spirit? For the old Greek, a tyrannical city
invaded the holy seclusion of the wise man.
For the new Roman, Caprice had ousted
Fortune from the throne; as for the natural
world, Chance ruled there. Domitian literally

forced an outburst of 'republican' sentiment; astrology only led evidence that " a harmony between fate and events " is dubious. Hence, personal independence took a fresh lease on life. Civilization was fatigued, honourable men were dejected and, if withdrawal proved impracticable save for the very few, all could contemplate the hallowed tranquillity of the sage, in Socrates, Diogenes, Brutus, Cato, and their kind, as the ideal haven. Much more than other Cynics whom we know, Epictetus was foremost among the very few.

Deus est mortali iuvare mortalem. Yes — but how? By adoption of Stoicism as a 'mission.' An apostle is demanded, one who has severed himself from " indifferent " affairs, — from family, dependents, vocation, civic duty, — for the express purpose of divining " things that are our proper concern, and things that are alien to us." He thus serves himself an ensample of the higher manhood, " a herald from God to men, declaring to them the truth about good and evil things; that they have erred, and are seeking the reality of good and evil where it is not; and where it is they do not consider. . . . A spy of the things that are friendly to men, and that are hostile; and having closely spied out all, he must come back and declare the truth. . . . His conscience giveth this power." [17]   But, to have found the ' way ' is by all odds more important than to enlist converts. Nay, no man may deliver his brother, seeing that the ' inner part ' abides utterly private. The sole good is a good will; the illuminated teacher can but declare the truth, leaving his disciples to reproduce it, each in his own order. Plainly, Epictetus embraces a pantheism of the internal spirit — every soul is a tiny fragment of God. The individual must discern this personally and, discerning, achieve his own proper tranquillity, so that Chance, Fortune, Fate, or whatever it is betides, can assail him not a whit. Thus the missionary, certain of his peculiar liberty, confines himself to stirring " the minds of his hearers toward the best things." He may not have souls to his hire, because each secret heart must be responsible for its own moral heroism. A consistent philosophy is out of the question, new effort hopeless, but some may lead *this* consistent life — " Sink into thyself, and rise redeemed."

Epictetus flouted theory. What Diodorus, and the followers of Panthoides and Cleanthes and Chrysippus held was no better than verbalism. " Show me, not persons who repeat the phrases of Stoicism, but a veritable Stoic, a man whose soul longs to be like-minded with God." [18] Bravely spoken; but the note rings out undisguised despair. He would evoke the moral aristocrat, self-justified by unbreakable stamina. Plainly, philosophy had become almost religion, not quite. Victory over sin and death is still doubtful; but the disinterested effort to govern self breeds a character that can afford, if not to defy the world and the things thereof like Seneca, then to neglect them, assured of a superiority infinite because internal. Spiritual pride, however chastened by the adventures of nigh five centuries, was the last, as it had been the first word of Cynicism. And the indispensable doctrine, its nobility notwithstanding, proved too high for those who must needs bear the burden and heat of common day.

The acrid tone of Quintilian's incidental references to philosophers, the Stoics conspicuously, may evidence professional jealousy or social prejudice.[19] None the less, it was characteristic of his day. Philosophy *had* brought unsettlement, and the 'wrangling schools' could not replace shaken faith. Then, too, Quintilian disliked its pretensions, he saw every reason why the orator, a 'practical' citizen, should be "the Roman wise man." But, the 'practical' was near the end of its rope. Perhaps under Trajan (98–117 A.D.), certainly under Hadrian and the Antonines (117–180 A.D.), another temper developed. Men grew more conscious, if not of the futility, then of the feebleness of thought; neither clever epigrams nor learned technical dispute about 'opinions' could gloss the fact. Happy by contrast with Nero's theatrical abominations or Domitian's lethal suspicion, the period suffered nameless apprehension, and intelligence retreated before the onset of occult powers. Not merely the 'vulgar throng,' but luxurious 'society,' and even the reflective few were suggestible to grovelling error. "The conflict of religions" marked a condition, concealed the cause, and the same may be said of Epictetus' 'inwardness,' tell-tale though both are. Whatever the case with Reason, the human soul was outgrowing ancient supports; even gracious Plutarch's "dear Apollo" breathes a pious sentimentalism, ineffectual because otiose. All dispensations had been tried and found wanting, men looked for a light shining in darkness. Marcus Aurelius has always shattered derogatory criticism, because his appeal to the resources of pure, selfless conscience is at once so sublime and so infinitely pathetic. Everything is transitory and frail, man most of all; and yet, somehow, the key to the mystery must be sought just where weakness seems superlative. Viewless this search may be, none other bears an iota of promise. The blameless conscience grapples the problem of problems unarmed save with its own idiosyncrasy, too scrupulous to cry for help. A religious interpretation of the world ensues, only to make manifest that the best soul is the most lonely.

"Foursquare and beyond the reach of blame," yet overborne by

> *" the weary weight*
> *Of all this unintelligible world; "*

such was Marcus Aurelius Antoninus. The man in the doctrine, not the doctrine *of* the man, has returned for reproof and uplift. He might be called Stoicism reviewing the

pageants of Nature and History. In any case,
his daily walk and conversations authenticated
his convictions. Lucian could affirm, " the
altars of Zeus are as cold as Chrysippus " —
religion is absurd, philosophy vacuous, therefore, let us enjoy the moment, eschewing
enthusiasms. The emperor knew better; a secret there must be. " Readiness for death can
proceed only from inward conviction, not come
of mere perversity, but of a temper rational
and grave, and unostentatious " (XI. 3). His
pensive melancholy sprang from the very circumstances that drew the hilarious levity of
Lucian. For, Marcus was truly the Last of the
Romans. Familiar with the assault of Greek
intellect upon the ' nature of things '; almost
persuaded that the ' Fortune ' of the empire
clinched monotheism; chief trustee of a law
coördinate with the natural order, and guaranteeing the inclusive unity of " a franchise by
mind and reason " (IV. 4), he yet sensed
vaguely the end of an age.

Nature seemed to revert to blind ' atoms '
and, if Roman experience reverted to gods,
they secluded themselves behind a Fate that
took small heed of individuals. But when thus
oppressed, Marcus Aurelius never boasted with

Horace, " I myself will provide the calm mind," the one thing needful. Rather, relying on a self-reverence beatified by reverence for others, he felt intensely that, when deliberate choice is right, everything mere man can do has been done. If all knowledge of Nature and all lessons of History speak in doubtful oracles, nothing can hinder a just man from planting both feet firm on his own conduct. " Either God works, and all is well; or, if all is random, be not thou too a part of the random " (IX. 28). " To vicissitudes caused from without, be imperturbable; in actions whose cause lies with yourself, be just — in other words, let impulse and act make social action their one end, and so fulfil the law of nature " (IX. 31). The chasm between aspiration and achievement defies bridging. But total defeat by the forces of the physical universe, complete disillusionment by the lapses of civilization, may be mitigated. Cycles of inevitable decay, and the disorders evacuated by human defect, *are* offset by personal loyalty to an internal spirit which no outer ill can touch, provided one be faithful. The Past may indeed condemn itself — Nature being indifferent or worse, and the slow-born devices of men

[70]

tainted by selfish passion; a reasonable government of the world eludes discernment.
Nevertheless, even granted that all details are
necessary evils, the true soul may reach out toward the "dear City of Zeus." Befriending
itself, it can befriend others, and thus portend
the Great Society. No instruments wrought
for its single purpose lie ready to hand. But
in very despite, contemplation of the implied
Whole consoles; all else must be suppressed
rigorously. "The soul becomes a 'self-
rounded sphere,' when it neither strains out-
ward, nor contracts inward by self-constriction
and compression, but shines with the light, by
which it sees all truth without and truth
within" (XI. 12). The gods of 'atoms' and
the God of the promise of immortality fall
apart. Faltering humanity would fain commit
itself to both, the emperor could commit himself to neither. "Supposing that translated to
some higher region you could look down upon
the world of man. . . . What food is here for
pride? . . . Reject the view — and straight-
way, you are whole" (XII. 24). This is Stoic
self-possession, victorious in submission. Purg-
ing away the braggart nonchalance of the
early Cynics, and the claim to indefeasible

personal liberty of his master Epictetus, Marcus Aurelius lived his message out. The sublimity of a self-poised character transcending a burden hardly to be borne, and recognizing itself the antechamber to something still more vast beyond, has won upon posterity. The high spectacle of tense conviction sufficed later pilgrims of the infinite, who have been content, accordingly, to forego curious inquiry about consistency in the doctrine.

Stoicism thus fixed its most influential type in an ethico-religious mood. This proved its last expression also. For, although the annalist Eutropius (*c.* 360) and others prize the example of Marcus Aurelius; although Julian ' the Apostate ' enlists Stoic precept to regenerate pagan society, not omitting to berate false Cynics; and although Simplicius (*c.* 529) commentates Epictetus, no fresh outgrowth appeared. Heroic virtue had done its best. The *æquanimitas,* given as the countersign to the tribune of the watch by the dying Antoninus Pius, implied a confidence in serene moral consistency identical with that which upheld Julian in face of death two centuries later.[20] From the time of Cicero, this Stoic mood had insinuated itself permanently into the ethical

outlook of the Roman governing groups.
Hence, for instance, it moulded the principles
of imperial jurisprudence from Nerva to Alexander Severus. In this way, being the keeper
of the Roman conscience, it passed over to
western civilization, an essential factor in the
main heritage bequeathed by the Empire.
Unable to captivate, it applied discipline and,
by rigid insistence on the absolute difference
between right and wrong, presaged a worthier
estimate of common humanity, equal in every
Roman citizen irrespective of race or previous
condition of servitude. It came nigh affirm-
ing that a man is primarily a soul to be saved,
quite aside from civic station or social duty,
and so prepared for the reception of Christianity. Nor did the relation stop short here.
" There is no doubt that a certain dimness of
vision accompanies temptation. . . . A man
must continually put his back to the wall, just
as in pain the hero determines through sheer
force of will to endure. . . . I should have
fallen if I had been able to rely for guidance
upon nothing better than a commandment. . . .
But the pure, calm, heroic image of Jesus
confronted me, and I succeeded." [21] When a
latter day Christian testifies thus, it is manifest that Stoicism, being dead, yet speaketh.

III. SOME STOIC DOGMAS

PLATO says: " We have certain *dogmata* concerning justice and good in which we were reared from childhood " (*Rep.*, VII. 538 C). One may set aside modern associations to retain the Greek term, because it conveys a precise meaning, neither more nor less. Literally an ordinance or, better, rule of life, the philosophers came to use ' dogma ' with Plato's intent. Hence, dogmas are statements of fundamental principle, definitive standards of a system. Although after Posidonius the Stoics laid less stress upon authoritative theory, yet the original view of the universe was never forsaken, and must be taken into account if we are to understand the permanent appeal of the School to the western mind. The reason is not obscure.

Before the individualistic schools began, the great constructive thinkers of Greece had completed their work. To employ a familiar phrase, they had covered the ground. Another system, thought out in one piece, was impossible, for knowledge was not destined to take an unforeseen sweep. Moreover, the literature of the first Stoics is a mere wreck, and we are thrown back upon indirect evidence, which may or may not do justice in detail. At the same time, two decisive facts are apparent. The Stoics attempted to frame a theory of the physical universe, of the individual man as he finds himself under compulsion in this universe and, combining the two, to formulate a rule of life in conformity with Reason. Approaching these problems in a new humanistic spirit, they suffused them with fresh and general interest. On the other hand, the several aspects of their teaching revert to previous philosophy, and although it would be unfair to allege that a mosaic resulted, the various elements lay side by side imperfectly unified. Like eclectics always, they forced contradictions to the point of paradox, and were inclined to save the day by appeal to practical considerations. Naturally, then, as the years passed and the first impulse waned, the theoretical dogmas, becoming more and more conventional, supplied a background for the ' art of life,' and the last stage was a deliberate watchfulness imposed by the known mysteries of the universe which remained insoluble, abashing rather than stimulating free inquiry. A *Weltweisheit* or popular moral philosophy, full of wise saws and modern instances, held the field.

Further, it should be remembered that the problems attacked by the Stoics arose from the political accidents of history, not from the orthodoxies or unorthodoxies of contemporary philosophy. As we have seen, the Greek type of state had served its generation, and was on the point of passage into the larger whole of empire. Thus, the question pressed, How is a man to reorganize values in face of the overthrow? "Bury me on my face," exclaimed Diogenes, "because, in a little while, all things will be turned upside down." Starting from the Cynic ideal of the Wise Man, the Stoics proceeded to amplify and reinterpret it, availing themselves at the outset of the results attained by Greek thought. The influence of the early cosmologists, of Socrates, the Megarians, and the Cynics dominates to begin with; Aristotle could not be forgotten and, with the Middle Stoa, Plato exerts fascination. But the whole perspective is altered. Accordingly, applying intellect to the moot points in true

Hellenic style, the Stoic sage, abandoning the old landmarks of citizenship, seeks to determine the nature of the strange world where he now finds his lot cast. As an immediate issue, he lights upon a bigger citizenship, inviting a cosmopolitan interpretation of conduct. In the previous section, we have tried to learn how later Stoicism developed this humanitarianism; the founders, and their distinctive ' dogmas,' claim attention here.

Secondary contrasts aside, peculiar unanimity pervades the Stoic view of philosophy. Physics, Logic, and Ethics divide the field. The relative stress laid on the first and second may have differed from time to time, the primacy accorded Ethics remained invariable. For a reason that may easily escape notice today, much attention was bestowed upon Physics in the formative stages of the School, while Logic, accounted little more than a method for exposure of fallacy, enjoyed least vogue. Although Ethics came at last to fill the entire foreground, it presupposed the dogmas of Physics, and necessarily. Ancient Physics took cognizance of problems now distributed among several sciences — astronomy, physics, biology, psychology, anthropology, natural theology, metaphysics, for example. Accordingly, it dictated the conditions determining wise conduct of life, supplied essential grounds why just this rule and none other must govern, and set forth some resources of the human being upon whom the application was incumbent. Ethics undertook the task of coördination.

The early Ionian cosmologists represented the scientific spirit as we understand it now. That is to say, they made it their business to trace the relations between physical phenomena, to the end that they might formulate an empirical generalization which, like the 'law of gravitation,' the 'nebular hypothesis,' or the 'evolution theory,' would suffice to 'explain' the known universe *within* its own terms. When one recalls the ceaseless activity during the two hundred and fifty years from Thales to Aristotle, it is fair to affirm that possible alternatives respecting the processes and constitution of Nature had been exploited. To this extent, then, the Stoics could but adopt current results. On the other hand, two additional movements had supervened since the cosmological period. It had become apparent that contrary inferences presented themselves even in theory of the universe. Thinkers might emphasize the superior importance of single phenomena, and come to pluralist or nominalist positions: on the other side, they might magnify the arrangement of the cosmos, the internal plan or unity, and rest in monist or realist convictions. In short, the 'Many' *or* the 'One' might well seem to offer the sole clue to the 'Whole.' It may be noted in passing that this formulation of alternatives has haunted scientific thought ever since. But a second movement deflected the course of inquiry even more. The decisive intervention of Socrates raised the anthropological problem, — Man, not Nature, is the proper study of mankind. It is all very well to allege, and even to prove, that an 'essence' permeates the passing show of the physical world. Even at the best, this concerns something over against man, something alien. Accordingly, it is much more important to determine whether there be a 'law,' independent of temporal change, governing the realm of local prescriptions, and national institutions. For, such a principle would be homogeneous with knowledge and, depending upon insight (*phronesis*), would result in self-control (*sophrosyne*). That is, knowledge of this law would of itself lead men to accept the good, and so ensure happiness.

Thus, apart altogether from the majestic systems of Plato and Aristotle, the Stoics found their stage set. The 'One' must be unified with the 'Many'; Nature must be brought into offensive and defensive alliance with Man; men as individuals must be aligned with Humanity, the universal. While, then, the factors of Stoicism are to be found in prior Greek thought, catastrophic secular events demanded their reorganization. Hellenism had run to contrasts and exclusions; the originality of Stoicism lies in its brave attempt to furnish inclusions, an imperative call from the circumstances of the age.

The social, ethical, and intellectual experience of Greece — unique in wealth and intensity — prompted the early Stoics to attack *the* problem which, more than any other perhaps, has beckoned reflective men everywhere. They sought to discover, even to guarantee, a primary relation between moral and natural law. The conclusions reached by Aristotle lent scant encouragement. Starting from sensuous objects, he had shown that the cosmic order can be traced to 'Matter' and 'Form' — indeterminate stuff, and a 'regular figure' bestowing arrangement. These, again, involved Potentiality and Actuality. As the Stoics saw the crux, such oppositions were fatal, the more that they suggested an irreconcilable difference between the world of sense and the world of intelligence. So far from falling apart, the two must be mutually supporting somehow or other; and, to sustain this view, it was necessary to deny alien 'passive matter' operated upon by 'active reason.' So the Stoics insisted that matter (or body), and nothing else, is capable alike of reception and origination of activity; it alone can be patient and agent. With this in mind, they abandoned the subtler analyses of the great systematists, and reverted to the broad, direct affirmations of the cosmologists and, probably, the physicians. Heraclitus of Ephesus (*c.* 540–470 B.C.) seems to have impressed them favourably. He had said: "Wisdom is one thing. It is to know the thought by which all things are steered through all things." "God is day and night, winter and summer, war and peace, satiety and hunger; but he takes various shapes, just as fire, when it is mingled with different incenses, is named according to the savour of each." These aphorisms are hard to understand. Presumably they mean that there is a ' One ' constituted by ' opposites,' and that the ' opposites ' are disclosed by self-division of the ' One.' What, then, was the ' One? ' " This order, which is the same in all things, no one of gods or men has made; but was ever, is now, and ever shall be an ever-living Fire, fixed measures of it kindling and fixed measures of it going out." Thus, abandoning Aristotle, and yet not flying too much in face of his authority, a dynamic principle and the things embodying it together constitute the homogeneous cosmos. But, the principle *belongs in* the cosmos — the reason for everything natural must be *in* Nature, that is, must be Nature, otherwise explanation of occurrences by reference to real causes would fail us. This original substance blazes up in all things, exciting them, so to speak. Yet, although it is sometimes called an ever-living Fire, as with Heraclitus, we must take this metaphorically, and think rather in terms of a tenuous breath, something elemental but not an element, something sublimated but not immaterial. The doctrine of Heraclitus was accommodated here to the idea of a restoring essence or power, which may have come down through Pythagorean medicine, to receive currency later from Hippocrates and his disciples. The Stoics are concerned to eliminate Platonic 'immaterial reals' even for the 'ultimate' which *is* Nature. They therefore declare that this ultimate must be known through bodily phenomena which share it. Things are a combination of the 'restoring essence' with something else — the conventional four elements in all likelihood. Thus, the original 'fiery Ether' is not perceptible in itself, but *is* experienced through sensible properties or 'perceived characters.' It manifests itself in an infinite series of phases, incidents of a hylozoistic process. Certain Stoics may have applied the term 'body' to human feelings and virtues, to the soul and to Zeus (god); even so, they were not materialists. They did not treat 'matter' as purely mechanical, nor did they derive natural, psychological, and spiritual phenomena from crass substance according to the universal operation of motion. The animism of the time led them to the notion of a vitalizing force that interpenetrates everything, and is the efficient cause of all happenings — the 'atmosphere-current' Reason of the world. It is but a step from this to Providence, Fate, Universal Law, Destiny, and the like; introduce these, and the Stoic Physics turns out a pantheistic hylozoism.[22] That is, we have a practicable basis for a parallelism between moral and natural law. How so?

In a universe thus organized, the primary quality of 'body' is tension, to be found at its utmost in the original Ether. Creative power (*spermatikos logos*) lies latent here. Evidently, then, all phenomena are conditioned by various degrees of tension, from the most tenuous and therefore intense, to the most inert and slackest. Eventually, too, motive-force runs down in the course of transformations, and must be restored by the reversion of all things to the primitive high tension Ether. Consequently, 'eternal return' lurks in the system of the universe, inseparable from its maintenance. A crisis must occur when the Many revert to the primigenous Activity and, when 'tone' has been reëstablished, the entire process will repeat itself. Some Stoics held that the catastrophe was marked by a universal conflagration, others demurred. But this doctrine is no essential part of the theory. The renovation may well be " effected by eternal exchanges," as Marcus Aurelius says. It suffices that " the lightning-flash of all-giving Zeus " refresh the enfeebled powers by " exchange of measures."

Within the terms of such a scheme, the human soul was conceived as a ' body,' its functions and qualities dependent upon states of tension. This admitted, it persists under the form of a simple rational activity which rules the dependent activities. As the Zeus-Ether governs the ' great world,' so the rational authoritative principle (*hegemonikon*) directs the ' little world ' of a human character. In both cases, the primitive tenuity permeates all possible events, retaining its own unity unbroken, however. Moreover, the human soul possesses the power to play this directive rôle because it is a part of the primitive ' world-soul.'

The antitheses left by the Platonic and Aristotelian philosophies are now superseded. ' Form ' and ' Matter ' no longer confront each other on opposite sides of a yawning gulf; nor Zeus and the World; soul and body;

psychical and physical states; free-will and fate; thought and sense; reason and volition. Monism ousts dualism and pluralism. Differences iron themselves out, as it were, thanks to the ascendancy of the 'germinative Reason,' manifest as organism in plants, as appetite in animals, as 'rational soul' — the " express image " of the Ultimate — in man. Moreover, on the theory, this 'soul' discharges tension in sensation, lends assent to judgments, impels itself toward desirable objects, thus developing through sensuous experience and intelligent discourse its proper nature, empty at the first. Feeling and knowing, its chief activities, are elicited as the physical world makes contact with them. So, sensations produce modifications within the mind, and these, in their turn, represent or symbolize objects. The presentations, named 'phantasies' (images) by the Stoics, are " affections occurring in the soul, revealing both themselves and that which caused them." Further, experience, or repetition, enables the soul to retain these 'phantasies,' so that it comes to harbour 'anticipations'; these, again, account for the group of ideas shared by all men mutually — 'common sense.' On this basis, conviction of truth must respond to a 'peculiar quality' in the object, and involve an unshakeable grip upon the actual. Thus, it would appear that all knowledge is acquired in the course of empirical events, but that the Reason which develops during the process is not produced by experience. In short, sensation 'goes in,' reason 'comes forth.' But, seeing the manifestation of the former depends upon the latter for effect, it is obvious that, as concerns conduct of life, Reason reigns supreme. To take a single comment; emotion is an "*irrational* and *unnatural* movement of the soul, or impulse in excess."

These and other technical 'dogmas,' while interesting to the special student of the history of ideas, are important in Stoicism primarily for their influence upon conceptions of the moral life and of man's relation to the urgent order of the universe. And, for our present purpose, the significance of the emphasis upon conduct is intensified by the fact that the imponderables of ethics and natural theology, rather than the exact methods of mathematico-physical research, have borne witness to its ubiquitous attraction down the ages.

It is more than probable that, from the outset, Stoicism missed the pure joy in scientific pursuit characteristic of Hellenic thought till Aristotle. Indeed, the consistent subordination of theoretical inquiry to Ethics intimates no less. Truth to tell, with the dissolution of the paramount claims exerted by the municipal state, the citizen felt acute need for "a medicine of the soul," as Cicero called it. Immemorial guidance gone, men sought a new guarantee within themselves. Yet, withdraw as they might, the world-order remained, a challenge. Reviewing the long struggle, Epictetus put the two aspects pointedly. "For as Zeus dwells within himself, and is tranquil by himself, and thinks of his own administration and of its nature, and is employed in thoughts suitable to himself; so ought we to be able to talk with ourselves, not to feel the want of others also, not to be unprovided with the means of passing our time; to observe the divine administration, and the relation of ourselves to everything else. . . When a man has this peace, not proclaimed by Cæsar, (for how should he be able to proclaim it?), but by God through reason, is he not content when he is alone? when he sees and reflects: ' Now no evil can happen to me; for me there is no robber, no earthquake, every thing is full of peace, full of tranquillity; every way, every city, every meeting, neighbour, companion is harmless'" (*Diss.*, III. 13). Self-control, in the sense of self-sufficiency, became the ideal, to be attained through self-knowledge and self-denial. Nevertheless, the "heavenly pattern seen in the Mount of God," to use Philo's phrase, loomed up, and self-sufficiency was shadowed by humble acquiescence in the mysterious ways of the cosmic Reason. That is, the moral demand had its religious side, and could not be separated completely from the problems of natural theology. This paradox, of a union between complete self-dependence and voluntary submission, intimates much.

Despite literary evidence to the contrary, ancient polytheism preserved vitality. One need go no further than the strange experience of Paul and Barnabas at Lystra for proof (cf. *Acts*, xiv). It is true that Gibbon's melodramatic description of the *Princeps*, — "a priest, an atheist, and a god," — had some slight basis in fact; by so much the more dread superstition flourished! Rooted for centuries in pride of race, in social usage, in

education, in dramatic ritual, in solemn com-
memorations, in humane art, in gracious
poetry, and in the whole structure of a
civilization deemed superior, the old religion
defied supersession for other centuries. A
middle class as we understand it did not exist.
And, if the cultured few fell upon easy scepticism or flippant indifference, they also bred
men of insight whom the sublime suggestions
of life and nature abashed or intrigued. As
for the masses, they stood in the ancient ways,
untouched by philosophical wiles, convinced
of aid from supernal powers, and therefore
capable of passionate fanaticism, as the early
Christians found.

Here, as in philosophy proper, the Stoics
practised ' accommodation,' contriving to align
their doctrines with popular faith, and ' allego-
rizing ' even crude beliefs, so as to include
them in the system. The religious tendency,
betrayed in Cleanthes' " Hymn to Zeus,"
waxed after Posidonius, gained mastery during the Pagan Reaction after Seneca, and left
distinct traces upon the development of
Hellenistic and Christian theology alike. Naturally, wide differences separated various
members of the school so that, in this connec-

tion precisely, we must speak of adjustment rather than of ' dogma.' Seneca's impatience, to say the least, of contemporary superstition, was one thing; the suspicious common-sense of Pliny the Elder, another; the occultism of his son, something else; the submission of Epictetus, haughtily humble, yet a fourth. Perhaps Galen (*c.* 180 A.D.), the whole movement behind him, may be taken as typical of the eclectic drift. An eminent physician, and a considerable figure in logic, his breadth qualified him to see all round a question. Thus, a thoroughgoing pantheist, he can have no traffic with the grosser delusions of the commonalty; praising Christians for their vigorous morality, — " some of them have gone so far that veritable philosophers could not surpass them," — he finds himself utterly at odds with their dogmatism; though inclined toward Plato, he is unable to concede an immaterial view of the soul. Moral and physical states are modes of one existence, and the soul a peculiar mixture of elements. So the alleged ' immaterial ' cannot be more than a form of harmony. Nevertheless, he finds it possible to rely on dreams for diagnosis and treatment, because fortunate results furnish empirical proofs. In short, his pantheism permits him to affirm the existence of the gods, his healing art attests the operation of providence, the invisible ally. The gods act as agents of providence, the primitive ' creator ' of the world. But the doctrine could work two ways. Accommodating itself to the cultivated who had no knowledge of technical philosophy, it could furnish room for ' dæmons,' or intermediaries, endlessly. On the other hand, the philosopher could salve consistency with the thought that the ' original ' god suffered just such limitations as the hard facts of nature seemed to imply. For example, " he has no power over the past except to cause it to be forgotten." Transcendental Reason fades into the background.

The future raised another issue. The world is " full of spirits," and yet all spirits, even the highest and most potent, are in bondage to Fate, the cycle of things. But Fate might be " read in the stars " which, thanks to their " heavenly eternity," reveal future purposes. The notion of the soul's " kinship with the stars " thus arose and, with it, the probabilism of immortality. Here, as in their theology, the Stoics spoke with uncertain sound. Some admitted an indeterminate existence after death; some held that the question could not be or, at all events, had not been settled; others, like Cicero, no doubt representing the temper of Stoic 'hearers,' deemed the soul 'divine' and therefore 'necessarily eternal' (*Tusc. Disp.*, I. 27). Death "brings to us, not extinction, but merely change of place" (*ib.* 49). The majority appear to have run the gamut between reluctant denial and vague hope. Seneca, for instance, oscillated in the course of his life, denying vigorously at first, stretching 'lame hands' wistfully at last to a "birthday of eternity." All things considered, it is evident that animism, with its corollary, belief in 'ghosts,' including discarnate spirits of the dead, produced deep emotional suggestibility. And, on the whole, it is fair to say that, in face of this popular mood, Stoicism took its own way.

The Stoics were well aware that the religious sentiment conferred benefits on men, but they also knew that it ran to paralyzing sentimentalities. Lack of speculative insight (or interest) clogged them here, however. They made no decision between monotheism and polytheism, because they never grappled the metaphysics of divine personality. Hence, it was simple for their looser adherents to refer all good in the universe to the 'creator,' all bad to lower gods or 'dæmons,' avoiding the ugly question of the responsibility of the principal for his agents. As Justin Martyr recounts, the Stoic did not know what God was, moreover he believed this knowledge superfluous. Now, men cannot rest in this dead centre. They ask for certainty that the 'gods' care, and for each soul apart. They seek "a Friend behind phenomena," and instinctively reject a cold Reason, oblivious of human risks. No need to say, the Stoics were human. In this strait, then, they fell back upon a doctrine of august lineage in Greek thought, of paramount significance, too, for the interpretation of the moral life. After all, Ethics, not Religion, was to enjoy preëminence. Stoic 'dogma' came to its own here.

Already, three generations ere Zeno taught in the Porch, the *Phædo* and *Symposium* of Plato had clothed upon "the heavenly pattern in the Mount of God." Socrates, idealized by the affection of his great disciple, stood forth a mortal linked with the divine. His austerity portended a detachment from earthly things whereby, escaping " the prison-house of the body " for a fair moment, he caught sight of the eternal verities. The separate soul is itself like a ' commonwealth,' haunted yet motivated by an ideal laid up in the heavens for him who desires to behold it and, beholding, found a city in himself (cf. *Rep.*, IX. 592 B). Conventionalizing the asceticism, and deeming that one might " found a city in himself " on irresponsible protest, the Cynics parodied Socrates. It remained for the Stoics, the later Stoics particularly, to redress the balance, and to disclose in the individual Wise Man a universal conscience, the divine spark in Humanity. Valiant in Greek intellectual confidence, the sage will unriddle existence and, transcending its " incurable insipidity," will justify it as the instrument of real virtue. Thus, dubiety about the gods led the Stoics to fall back upon the ancient Hellenic apotheosis of men who, by superior personality, had abolished the gulf between the divine and the human. The choicest of these choice spirits was no conquering satrap, not even a beneficent law-giver, but the hero in common life, virtuous by sheer decision of character.

In Pauline language, the Stoics were " a law

unto themselves . . . their conscience also bearing witness " (*Romans*, ii. 14, 15). Moral sense, and strength to obey were natural faculties, enabling them to judge and select action. Personal insight and conviction held the essence of the matter. The ' gods ' might safeguard the moral law *post factum*. But, good and, more emphatically, evil, depend upon human decisions. As the " Hymn " of Cleanthes has it:

> " *The universal Logos flows through all* . . .
> *Save what the sinner works infatuate.*"

Following hard upon Cynicism, the early Stoics press this independence. The Wise Man, though in the body and the world, is above them, being indifferent to the assaults of passion and chance. He *will* not submit to ' impulse,' indeed *can* not, when the light of Reason shines clear. Pleasure, desire, anxiety, fear, the four horsemen of the apocalypse of pathological disturbance, are ' unnatural.' And, knowing how to ' live in accord with Nature,' the Wise Man escapes them, being ' healthy.' Proper judgment, identical with ' virtue,' places him in position to elect whether he will be unshaken by inward impulse or outer circumstances. So Zeno could declare: "In all things is the divine; the law of nature is divine; the fulfilment of a man's life is to live in accord with nature; virtue of itself is sufficient for happiness; and things that are neither good nor evil are indifferent; and things indifferent are these — life and death, good repute and ill repute, pain and pleasure, riches and poverty, sickness and health, and such like. And of men there are two sorts, the upright man and the wicked man. Only the wise, however ill-favoured, are beautiful; for the lineaments of the soul are more beautiful than those of the body."

The underlying 'dogmas' are thus comparatively simple. Morality is an affair of 'the inward part.' This, again, consists in a 'rational nature' common in origin with the Reason that creates and rules the cosmos. A universal 'law' therefore uplifts men above circumstances in such fashion that, if it be discerned, the sole evil possible is disobedience. Hence, the worst mischances as the average account them, even suffering, material disaster, and death itself, are quite 'indifferent.' They hold no power to harm any soul true to itself. As a result, the 'whole duty of man' may be summed in two brief precepts: submission to the Providence or Fate governing the world, and realization of 'the divine spark within.' Both, once more, ensue upon developed exercise of natural insight. On the whole, the earlier Stoics seem to have thought in terms of the first precept, emphasizing adjustment to the ultimate course of things and, with it, the idea of a cosmopolitan community inclusive of all men, as against the particularism of the Hellenic cities. Of course, this presupposed philosophical knowledge and grasp. Accordingly, they divided the sheep from the goats contemptuously. There was a very select group of the " excellent and altogether comely " (*spoudaioi*), healthy in a wisdom thoroughly conscious of the irremediable opposition between the reasonable and the 'unnatural.' The great mass was 'of no account' — perfectly 'trivial and worthless' (*phauloi*). For, despite fidelity to the ordinary decencies, they were hopeless failures ethically. From this point of view, all conventional observances and institutions became 'indifferent,' a *doctrinaire* idealism expelling every merit from customary morality.

It were superfluous to dwell on the weakness

of these 'dogmas'; Christian apologists have
made the most of it! As with rigorism always,
there is overmuch nourishing of self on its own
substance; resultant spiritual pride hinders
sympathy and coöperation; exceptional intelligence forms a prerequisite to goodness, making the common man merely worthless;
indifference lets opportunity slip and, in the
long run, cramping the soul, impoverishes it.
Inevitably, 'escape,' the final cause of life,
being of and by the best, stands self-condemned
as treason to all. Push Stoicism to the extreme
of its Cynic implications, then its "world is
the best of all possible worlds, and everything
in it is a necessary evil;" and, "where all is
rotten it is a man's work to cry stinking fish."
Nay, more. Given a deaf and dumb deity, the
theory ends in apotheosis of personal reason,
and each individual becomes his own god.
Posing as the new 'uplift,' at a time when
Greek institutions were in the melting-pot,
this Stoicism might be urged for a little under
the abnormal conditions. But, when empire
steadily displaced municipality, and when the
Roman deflected the Hellenic spirit, radical
alterations ensued. And, at last, the Stoicism
destined to join the main stream of western

culture was no helpless counsel of perfection, but the *one* pagan mood which, by bringing men into coercive relations with large impersonal issues, enabled and emboldened them to live on the higher level *within* their own world. The two moods, such is their persistence, find concentrated expression even in the most recent verse. Sure of himself, the Stoic pioneer flouts with

> *" It is one to me that they come or go . . .*
> *Let them think I care, though I go alone,*
> *If it lifts their pride, what is it to me*
> *Who am self-complete as a flower or stone? "*

Chastened by the insistent realities of life, later Stoicism muses:

> *" But we have lived enough to know*
> *That what we never have remains;*
> *It is the things we have that go."* [23]

This softening of ' dogma ' bespoke fuller insight.

It is easy to carp at a ' double standard ' in knowledge and conduct, less easy to follow the transformation of Stoic ' dogma ' from abstract theory to practicable counsel. For, although bent to the demands of the time, the theory never vanishes. The treatment of that cardinal tenet, virtue, affords an excellent illustration of the process. Theoretically, virtue must be single — self-consistent, self-contained. Indeed, high-minded devotion to elevated purpose (*phronesis*) alone is virtue. Greek tradition justifying, one might paraphrase the term as ' conscious elevation of mind,' where ' mind ' covers the entire disposition, and stress falls on the ' conscious ' — approving personal awareness. But, the most elevated disposition misses effect unless it find forthright opportunity. Recognizing this, the later Stoics taught that the temper may be manifested in many ways, conspicuously in the other cardinal virtues distinctive of the Hellenic *ethos:* tactful reasonableness, honourable fortitude, blamelessness. Similarly, it may step down to lower levels. Admit this, and the pure unity of virtue has been flecked by non-virtuous intrusions.

> " *Life, like a dome of many-coloured glass,*
> *Stains the white radiance of eternity.*"

Important consequences follow, especially for the doctrine of the Wise Man. After all, How are *we* to live? Seneca replies: "We ought to choose some good man, and always have him before our eyes that we may live as if he watched us, and do everything as if he saw." But, where is the paragon to be found — of single eye in purpose, of imperturbable serenity? The heroes of the race, Socrates himself no exception, have come short of this. Hence, the sharp division of mankind into *perfect* sages and *perfect* idiots must be abandoned. Even the best have shown and show weakness, history and contemporaries attesting. The invincible self-sufficiency of the real sage neither is nor has been attained. So it is necessary to recognize steps forming as it were a ladder from the perfect fool up to the near-wise. Many halting practitioners of virtue there be, and even of the 'proficient' we may affirm only that he is 'far gone' in virtue (*prokoptōn*). Nay, it is possible to detect a savour of good in the 'legal' conscience. For, if elevated disposition play no part here, there is at least politic adjustment to affairs of real practical moment. A man may serve the right obliquely, by giving "no offence to one who is more powerful " — the emperor, for example.

Plainly then, virtuous activity, so far from being peculiar to the ' inward part,' comes into contact with worldly things, and the question of preference arises forthwith. How can the righteous man keep conscience clear *and* palter with concessions to a corrupt society? The Stoic dream of a cosmopolis " in which the cities of men are as it were houses," suggested one way. Perchance, the present order portends the advent of the ideal commonwealth and, if a man serve dutifully, he may hasten the ' great year.' But the far-off divine event, the City of Zeus, could appeal only to the fit few. Accordingly, the Stoics met the problem for the many by weighing *pros* and *cons*. The things of this evil world might be graded. Thus, some may stand ' preferred,' because meet or proper to present conditions in mundane affairs. Situated as they are, men may approve skill, reputation, noble birth, and even personal beauty, reckoning them ' fortunate ' aids. Other things may be judged ' indifferent '; Reason must decide whether, under its power of choice, they can be brought to bear genially on the moral state. Life itself, for instance, may be so beset by obstacles as to become ' indifferent,' and Reason may conclude that, to preserve virtue, the ' open door ' (suicide) must be taken. So it came about that the business of Philosophy was to furnish rules for special cases; it undertook a hortatory function, recommending the more excellent way, advising the weaker vessel. In short, the ' dogmas,' while never abandoned in principle, gave immediate place to maxims for guidance in ordinary contingencies, and became relative to fluctuating circumstances. It was essential only to encourage intent of well-doing, and by advice capable of rational defence.

Finally, the ' dogma ' of ' Nature ' altered its centre of gravity, so subtly too, that the transformation seems to have escaped the Stoics themselves, — their critics sensed it. " Life according to Nature " had implied " according to Fate," which allotted or decreed human destiny in ways past finding out, nay, often, past justification. Job's question returned for judgment. " What? shall we receive good at the hand of God, and shall we not receive evil? " The Stoics neither faced it nor forsook their theoretical determinism. The unstable equilibrium could not maintain itself. ' Nature ' came more and more to imply human nature — an organization with an insight, preferences, and a chief end of its own. The grim, doubtful figure of Fate assumed the kindlier lineaments of Providence, a spirit endued with forethought, working advisedly for purposes *within* human estimate of righteousness. Briefly, emphasis shifted from the ' ought to be ' to the ' is '; morality, content to labour for an elusive adjourning realization, was replaced by the conviction that, somehow, the consummate has guarantee in the amplitude of human nature. Membership in the perfect whole has thus been taken by assault, and we have — Religion. Almost, not quite! "Zeus hath placed by the side of each a man's own Guardian Spirit, who is charged to watch over him . . . To this god you also should have sworn allegiance, even as soldiers unto Cæsar. . . . And what oath will you swear? . . . Never to murmur at aught that comes from his hand: never unwillingly to do or suffer aught that necessity lays upon us." So Epictetus preached. Hear Marcus Aurelius also: " I am in harmony with all that is a part of thy harmony, great Universe . . . Let us accept such orders, as we do the orders of our

Æsculapius . . . He who knows not the world-order, knows not his own place therein. And he who knows not for what he exists, knows not himself nor the world . . . To my moral will my neighbour's will is as completely unrelated as his breath is or his flesh. Be we ever so much made for one another, our Inner Selves have each their own sovereign rights. . . . It rests now with me, that within this soul of mine there be no vice, nor desire, nor any perturbation at all; perceiving the true nature of all things, I use each at its proper worth. Remember this prerogative is yours by nature." Reason still gives man pause. The Ruling Power, personal in Epictetus' Guardian Spirit, personal in Marcus himself, is impersonal in the Universe. Religious certainty flickers, for " Death is " not " swallowed up in victory." Just pride in identity with a perfect being alternates with a resignation to sightless Fate, so sublime in its loyalty to Reason as to hush comment, so pathetic in its final abandonment of a near hope as almost to persuade that a consuming passion may bemuse rather than certify. And, when consuming passion is out of the question, this phase of the Stoic temper cannot but revive in far other worlds, under far other skies.

IV. SEQUELS

AS we saw at the outset, Stoicism lacks originality and, even more, internal self-consistency. No Stoic can be ranked among the major thinkers, nay, the members of the School taken as a group add little to the resources of technical philosophy. Nevertheless, as we also saw, the movement must be reckoned among the factors constitutive of the moral and cultural atmosphere of mankind, in the western world especially. Evasive, it has proven remarkably pervasive, except perhaps in the other-worldly aspiration of the Middle Ages, and even then its traces remain. The apparent paradox may disappear if we recall that Stoicism adjusted itself to a mood or, rather, moods of the human spirit bound to recur in the nature of the case. Its very looseness lent it adaptability. For, consider, it embodied a theory of the universe dependent upon brave, rational acceptance of things as they are, in the conviction that, somehow, reason can come to terms with the world-order. Accordingly, it has appealed permanently to all for whom, no matter what the momentary condition of science, " knowledge has ripened into meditation, and has prompted high desire." No further proof were necessary than that eloquent pronouncement by Mr. Bertrand Russell, " A Free Man's Worship." [24] This intellectual appeal, savouring of Greek personal integrity, must always attract the awakened mind, true to its own clear conclusions. But, second, Stoicism bred a tonic morality, nurtured on self-examination, and rendered tense by self-discipline. As Apuleius (*c.* 125–174) says: " One must cherish his disposition reverently, for there is nothing more like unto God, nor more acceptable in His sight, than a man upright in perfect sincerity." Indeed, should ' natural knowledge ' abolish God, this man could still captain his own soul, certain that, whatever he did, he could do none other: and if, happily, ' convicted ' of the grace of God, he could remove mountains. In Renan's words, " this gospel . . . belongs neither to one race nor to one country. No revolution, no progress, no discovery will have power to change it." Skies may vary endlessly, this *animus* persists

imperishable. Numerous and contrasted manifestations attest it. The shy saintliness of
Thomas à Kempis (c. 1380–1471), when half
Europe travailed with that inward tendency
of Christianity which surveys the individual
soul and its relations to God, lends one illustration. The "private exercise of mind" convinced of a direct call from God, sustaining
and chastening the Friends (Quakers), bodes
the same mood. So does Matthew Arnold,

"*With close-lipped Patience for my only friend,*"

and even Mrs. Meynell, intent upon "bare
thoughts shapely with their own truth." The
Ethical Culture Movement in our own more
secular time revives the temper somewhat dif-
ferently and, but yesterday, the newest phase
found vigorous expression in the ringing words
of Carl Hauptmann: "It is perverse to believe that the individual is nothing, the State
everything. It is in truth just the opposite.
There is only one authority, that of the invisible god within us." Thus Stoicism has survived on the one hand in a theory which swings
all the way between hopeless yet pathetic or
defiant recognition of natural law, and a mystic suspicion that, despite temporal mischance,

the very stability of the 'eternal return' may portend a 'Divine Friend.' On the other hand, it has vivified the dignity of the man who, sure of the approval of his own conscience, can govern his private self — a glorious realm, — or, by the same sign, can account himself peculiarly worth the special aid or favour vouchsafed by infinite Grace. And, granted that theology, theoretical or moral, be the single reading of the universe comprehensible by the average, we have two most powerful motives necessarily inexpugnable from life. Theoretical they may be in large part, but theory is not all, and the Stoics hit upon a practical problem not a whit less inevitable.

Men dwell together in political communities and, given due fortune, may contrive a union able to preserve and enlist their best qualities. The Greek municipal state achieved this free authority in its high hour, so much so that the citizens found it the source and guarantee of the 'spiritually indispensable.' Thus, keenly aware of their privileges, they felt that an impassable gulf yawned between them and " lesser breeds without the law." But on the advent of empire, virtue leaked away, particularism grew impracticable, and a new adjustment became imperative. Travelling a third line, Stoicism stepped into the breach with a cosmopolitan creed: men are born equal by nature, and owe allegiance, not to the parochial regulations of petty towns, but to that universal law which "appears with the beginnings of the rational creation, and remains unchangeable." The private individual, urbane or uncouth as the case might be, was led to appreciate or assert himself, raising fresh issues destined to ring down the centuries. Hence, the question of the 'unalienable rights' of personality challenged decision and, with it, the no less thorny problems of the ground and justification of sovereignty in civil societies. For, obviously, the doctrine of natural equality implies that *each* human being enjoys an inherent capacity to exercise political judgment quite apart from the dower conferred by folk-consciousness. So, whether we hold that social institutions follow upon man's fall from a pristine condition of innocence, being bad at the best, or that they are inseparable from the 'political animal,' the conflict between rights and duties, between private inviolability and public subordination, has burst forth. On these supremely practical issues, with whatever injection of theory, Stoicism was fated to guide or, at least, to haunt the western world for many a long day.

In sum, then, the flexible tenets of Stoicism trafficked with the three fundamental aspects of human life. What is man's relation to, what his portion in the physical universe? What are one's obligations to the ' inner law ' of the heart when confronted with other laws disapproved by conscience, or, how surmount the crisis of ' a divided duty ' ? What are a man's veritable ties with his neighbours in view of the necessity for politico-economic organization and the reasonable claims incident to his personal self-respect? Now, these happen to be precisely *the* permanent questions pertaining to what we may term spiritual guidance. One or another may lack urge for a little, the three seldom subside together. And seeing that, no matter with what inconsistency, Stoicism was first afield in meeting all, it is small wonder that in successive ages and in very divergent circumstances, its solutions and, more insinuating, its suggestions, exerted manifold, sometimes potent influence. Volumes might be devoted to the gradual annealing of western civilization; to the emergence of the systems

of Latin Christianity and Feudalism, and to
the dissociation of their elements in the ferment
of the Renaissance and Reformation. We must
content ourselves with the merest sketch here,
tracing the aftermath of Stoicism. This done,
we shall turn for a moment to our own troub-
lous day, — 'a period of retrenchment' ex-
hibiting phases curiously similar to those which
found vent in cosmological and ethical Stoicism,
therefore ordained to evolve kindred moods.

1. THE LARGER FRAMEWORK

It might be affirmed that Stoicism, its service
done, fell from power after the death of Marcus
Aurelius. Just as the early cosmological system lapsed long ere the Roman Stoics, just as
Seneca went into eclipse before the reign of
Domitian, so even the religious stage of the
movement waned toward the close of the
second Christian century. In a fashion, nothing could be truer and — more misleading.

A great churchman — for this very reason
critical of the Stoics — found himself compelled to declare: " It is difficult to estimate,
and perhaps not very easy to overrate, the extent to which Stoic philosophy had leavened the

moral vocabulary of the civilized world at the time of the Christian era." [25] As is recognized now, the generalization may be extended to Christianity itself. For, while it is true that oriental worships mainly of Syrian and Egyptian origin, emphasizing the need for direct communion with *some* deity as a guarantee of personal immortality, came to oust Stoicism, it is also true that Stoic ideas penetrated the combination of factors absorbed in the Christian system after a coalescence requiring a long three centuries. In all likelihood, it will never be possible to adjudicate details with confidence, especially for primitive Christianity. Everyone knows the remarkable parallels between Seneca and St. Paul, the coincidences between the *Gospels* and Epictetus. Information failing, it is the part of caution to trace them to common sources in the whole circle of ideas, emotions, and desires of Hellenistic culture then in rapid process of change. At all events, the similarity is there, and one may heighten or minimize it according to prepossession. On the other hand, when the early phase of plaintive or plangent emotion had receded, becoming a tale that was told, and when Christians took stock of their faith, a more or less

learned defence grew imperative. Nay, apart
altogether from the ebb of the original onset
of feeling, the steady accession of educated
(therefore Greek-speaking) converts wrought
a new outlook insensibly.

It must be insisted, and never forgotten,
that Christianity had a *vivida vis* all its own,
and in two ways at least. First, Philosophy
had moved toward monotheism with widespread effect. Maximus Tyrius (*c.* 190) and
Eusebius (*c.* 300) agree that, for gentle and
simple alike, the old national gods were assist-
ants or children of the one God, ' king over all.'
But this deliverance from polytheism, its prev-
alence despite, fell short of revelation. Christianity furnished the historical revelation of
God seeking men out — the Divine Life had
been made manifest, and not to a mere fortunate few: all *could* be won and regenerated by
the Friend who sticketh closer than a brother.
Second, the strong Hebrew element in the new
religion evoked spiritual things hitherto strange
to the Græco-Roman world. Take St. Paul,
whose Tarsian associations so exposed him to
Stoicism and to the mystery-religions that it is
impossible to assess their influence even yet.
His anthropology, pivoting on the conflict be-

tween ' Flesh ' and ' Spirit,' is drawn from the Old Testament, not from Plato or from contemporary platonizing teachers. His doctrine of Election roots in an idea absolutely fundamental to Jewish literature and history. His conception of Sin as disobedience to the Divine Will, with consequent need for atonement, is altogether alien from the Hellenic consciousness. While his philosophy of history, with its three essential moments typified in Adam, Moses, and Christ, is Hebraic enough to call for no comment. Nevertheless, admitting this originality of the new faith or, if you prefer, pressing it to the point of ' uniqueness,' norms and valuations distinctive of Greece and Rome did find entrance into the Christian system; and, though the decisive ideas be traceable to the genius of Plato, Stoicism played its part also.

To make assurance doubly sure, let us go a step further and, citing Plutarch, convict the Stoics of " savage and hard apathy; " or, admonished by the outbursts of certain apologists, recognize the " lofty disdain," the " utter insufficiency for a hungering soul," — the whole reading of existence being " the offspring of despair," and " little more than an epitaph on

the ideal of ancient life." Or, again, neglecting
for the moment an inexplicable misapprehension of the Greek standpoint, let us allow the
" shocking blasphemy " of Chrysippus when he
said: " the wise man is as useful to Zeus as
Zeus is to the wise man." [26] And, lest these
detractions be insufficient, let us frankly declare that, under the Empire, many who wore
the Stoic garb made it a cloak for " hectoring
insolence," for anti-social humbug, and, in one
conspicuous instance at least, for " captious
malice." Still, even this catalogue of enor-
mities, alleged or real, affects not a whit the
patent fact that Stoicism had much to do with
shaping the larger framework of western
civilization.

It would be quite misleading to suggest that
disciples of a Stoic system are to be found down
the ages. Till Augustine and, thereafter, till
Augustinianism was absorbed in Scholasticism,
Plato, read in the light of Neoplatonism, exerts
the greatest influence by far. At the same time,
Stoicism continues to make two appeals. Its
hylozoic pantheism, modified by certain mystic-
magical tendencies, and its moral idealism win
many. Here the sources are literary rather
than philosophical in the technical sense. Vir-

gil, Cicero, Seneca, and, to a lesser extent, Epictetus and Marcus Aurelius, enlist admiration or stimulate trains of thought. On the whole, too, especially as Christianity develops its distinctive solutions, the pantheism acts negatively, the moral idealism positively.

The adjustments productive of a Christian system were prolonged through several centuries; the *fiunt, non nascuntur Christiani* of Tertullian cannot date much before 200 A.D. During this fluid period, the universalism, cosmopolitanism, and humanitarianism of the Stoics exerted immense leverage; curious as it may seem, even their pantheism and rationalism filled a gap. Take the latter. A soul might seclude itself, intent upon the way of salvation. But, the universe and society are here, asserting some minimal claim, and nobody could altogether evade the question of his relation to them. If in another way, the Christian was bound to face the order of Nature just as Lucretius did: " When we look up to the great expanses of heaven, the aether set on high above the glittering stars, and the thought comes into our mind of the sun and the moon and their goings; then indeed in hearts laden with other woes, that doubt too begins to awake

[118]

and raise its head — Can it be perchance, after all, that we have to do with some vast divine power that wheels those bright stars each in its course? " Accordingly, a cosmology was demanded; and the Stoic in Philo lent such convenient aid that we owe the transmission of many writings of this great eclectic to his popularity with the Fathers of the Church. Briefly, a ' natural religion ' was implanted by Stoicism in Christianity, so much so that Justin Martyr had the boldness to entitle his faith a " philosophy," Jesus a " teacher " (sophist) no less than a saviour. In a word, the *Christian* Roman citizen, possessing no theory of his own, borrowed one whence best he might. Moreover, when it came to details, he could not but be struck by the similarity between many maxims learned at the family altar and the " Sayings " of the Master heard in meeting. He had no authoritative church, no canonical books, no stated body of doctrine to supply unexceptionable guidance; nay, Christian views themselves, as they passed from mouth to mouth or travelled from congregation to congregation, assumed variable colour and emphasis. Nothing had been thought through. For instance, how was the believer to connect divine unity

[119]

with his own selfhood, or divine righteousness
with a personal God such as mere man might
conceive? Emphatically, a theory of relations
must be discovered to stiffen, as it were, mere
efflux of emotion, and to ward off the clever
assaults of pagan dialectic. This theory formulated itself in Greek and, perforce, retained
Greek modes of thought. Even the authority
of the Old Testament was supported and rendered intelligible by Greek exegesis, as the
fragments of the ' Apology ' of Aristides show
quite early (*c*. 130). And, seeing that Stoic
eclecticism was the principal philosophy, it
offered a large part of the needful theory ready
to hand. Thus the *dogmata* (in the usage
current among the Greek philosophical sects)
of the " Christian Philosophy " came into being. They absorbed the Stoic *Logos,* the Stoic
moralism, and the Stoic-Philonian allegorical
method which, in combination with Platonic
metaphysics and dualism, were applied to in-
terpret the " Sayings " of Jesus familiar from
congregational lectionaries, and the pious " ex-
hortations, rebukes, and sacred censures " of
preachers, as Tertullian calls them. In short,
a system was evolved — impossible without
Stoicism. Indeed, Græco-Roman philosophy

remained the quarry for 'secular' knowledge through a millenium. So much for the pantheism and the rationalism.

When it comes to universalism, cosmopolitanism, and humanitarianism, the most hidebound critics are ready to feature the rôle enacted by Stoicism in "the Preparation for Christianity." But, this is not enough. Taken together, these inseparable conceptions not only foreshadowed the Evangelical outlook, but furnished it a standpoint — framework with facts. Alexander the Great may have been a general of genius; his real importance roots in his abolition of the circumstances which divided Greek from Barbarian, Jew from Gentile, and, eventually, Roman citizen from subject alien. In the same way, Frederick II (1194–1250) may have been the "wonder of the world, in mere accomplishments the greatest prince who ever wore a crown;" his real importance roots in the impetus he gave to alignments wherein nations were to arise once more. Between the two, Stoic cosmopolitanism had free course. The universe is a single whole, governed by a single Reason, and men are scions of a single race, bound in a single brotherhood. Zeno's "one flock feeding in

one pasture " is a vision no more when the
Roman Empire, the foretaste, has been sup-
planted by the City of God on earth, the
Church Catholic. Plainly enough, if mankind
be one, and if the world of their habitation be
one, then the common unity, the overruling
Power, must flow as freely through things as
through souls. " I cannot find it in my heart
to be angry with any *man*, for we are all made
for mutual help, as the feet, the hands, the
eyelids." Such was the cosmopolitanism of
Marcus Aurelius. If so, then ultimately the
human spirit, in its obligations and destiny
alike, must revert to some universal guidance
and, seeking, find it in a cosmopolitan organization. Further, with the universal Empire
as theorised and supervised by Stoics at actual
work in Rome, this all-inclusive community
of perfectionists was bound to take no account of race or place, but solely of its
peculiar œcumenical function. " He cannot
have God for his father who has not the Church
for his mother," as Cyprian (*c.* 240) was among
the first to see. The Stoic City of Zeus had
descended from heaven to dwell among men.
Thanks in no secondary measure to Stoic universalism, cosmopolitanism, and humanitari-

anism, Catholic and Roman became identical, and means were devised which transformed the lives of millions *after* the "*disappearance* of Stoicism*" !* What irony! Truth to tell, Stoicism was absorbed in and, eventually, transcended by the Christian system.

As if this were not sufficient, it has been suggested that "Stoicism influenced Christian views of God and society too much." [27] Omitting the theological aspect, note that Stoicism formulated distinctive moral doctrines, sometimes with much psychological subtlety. There can be little doubt that a rigorist party flourished among primitive Christians, and that Montanism (*c.* 156) was a reversion to this survival of Jewish legalism. There can be little doubt, too, that Monasticism (*c.* 350), whatever its origin and development, represented kindred tendencies intensified, probably, by oriental dualism. But, making every allowance for the control exercised by these early and later movements, it is certain that the Stoic *mens conscia recti* became part and parcel of popular Christian teaching. I suppose this is what Nietzsche implied in dubbing Seneca "the toreador of virtue." When the apostle thundered forth, " By

[123]

the deeds of the law shall no flesh be justified in His sight . . . but now the righteousness of God without the law is manifested," he turned a whole world upside down. For, either a higher law, apt to be too hard for human frailty, will prevail, or, considering the backslidings yet decent impulses of the average,

" *Men who can hear the Decalogue, and feel*
No self-reproach,"

can be trusted to govern their conduct according to honourable custom touched by insight. The impossibilities of the one will invite continuous divine interposition — " with God all things are possible; " the other will accrue from natural ability to choose the good. In the nature of the case, Stoicism taught the latter and, in so doing, not only contributed a permanent factor to Christianity, but planted the seeds of several stimulating controversies. The ideas of the great Cappadocian Fathers, Gregory Nazianzen (*c.* 330–390) and Gregory of Nyssa (*c.* 332–395), about the ability of the ' natural ' will to work with God unto salvation, and about the consequent " universal restoration " of all men, offer cases in point alike for the ancient and the contemporary worlds. It was

really a question between the " New Law,"
inseparable from a supernatural righteousness
pendent upon withdrawal from the " flesh,"
and Græco-Roman " virtue " attainable in a
" life according to nature."

No doubt, while on the crest of the first
enthusiasm, perfection by bearing " the complete yoke of the Master " seemed the sole
ideal. This conviction was reinforced, too,
by the doctrine of universal righteousness in-
tegral to the " Second Coming " as then believed. But, by the beginning of the second
century, accommodation to the pressure of social affairs, and to ineradicable Roman custom,
had supervened. If men find it impossible to
maintain the higher level, then let them do
what they can, so the *Teaching of the Twelve
Apostles* counselled (*c.* 120). And, what might
this practicable ' second best ' be? One need
go no further than Justin Martyr (*c.* 150), Minucius Felix, and Clement of Alexandria (*c.*
200) to discover.[28] The pure Stoicism of Clement's *The Instructor* witnesses the adoption into
Christianity of the most honourable teaching
of reflective heathenism. Justin's doctrine of
freedom holds for Socrates no less than for
Christian saints: " we teach some things like

[125]

the Greeks." In short, Stoicism is grafted upon the Christian view of conduct once for all. Not without protest. Tatian (*c.* 170), in one way, Tertullian (*c.* 200) in another, with which the premillennarian stress upon exceptional righteousness had much to do, enter strenuous objection to the 'lapse,' setting Christianity and paganism by the ears. While Clement can regard philosophy as a " schoolmaster " to bring the Greeks to Christ, Tertullian must needs denounce *miserum Aristotelem* and his " destructive " dialectic. Stoicism was not preoccupied with the doctrine of " Last Things," but with this present dubious life and how to render it tolerable. Neopythagorean and other apocalyptic visions drawing Tatian and Tertullian aside from the main stream, Stoicism was not for them. Still they fought their fight. Gnosticism and Montanism left deep marks, thanks to their practical interest, — it *was* something to be rid of " the world-rulers of this darkness," or to achieve conduct fitting self for partnership with Christ. Hence, the Christian ascetic deemed the Greek ideal of " measure " or moderation in practice beneath contempt, no better than damnable treason. The conflict waxed till the second half of the fourth century, when the old Roman *virtue*, kept alive by a splendid tradition and the system of education, exerted determining, indeed, final influence, thanks to those great personalities, Jerome and Augustine. Deeply versed in the Hebrew Scriptures, Jerome was saturated with Cicero and Virgil. Cicero had much to do with giving direction to Augustine, and Virgil pervades the *City of God*. Philosophy had fallen upon evil days, as Jerome asserts, and as the popular, if extraordinary, manual of *The Seven Liberal Arts* by Martianus Capella proves. But this same philosophy, attested now by revelation, treated the profound things with luminous objectivity, thanks to Augustine. Nay, even the *Confessions,* despite their tincture of Gnostic dualism, sound the abysses of *humanae conscientiae* — a Stoic conception. At the same time, Augustine was no pagan, because he lifts the soul to a living Infinite. Yet, the example of Ambrose (*c.* 390), the last veritable Roman, had told its tale.[29] *Profani si quid bene dixerunt non aspernandum.* In sum, then, matters so transpired that it were futile to " reason high "

" Of *providence, foreknowledge, will, and fate,*
  Fixed *fate, free will, foreknowledge absolute,*"

without taking Stoicism into constant account. At the dawn of the Christian era Manilius had already struck the chord destined to be a dominant in the Augustinian symphony. "Who could know heaven save by heavenly grace, or find God if he were not himself a part of God?" Because the Stoa made philosophy *moral* philosophy and, at the same time, linked it with profound speculative problems, no limit can be set to its leaven within the undivided Church. The quotation above from Milton suggests the return to Stoic 'inwardness' in certain aspects of Protestantism. The results may have been good, they may have been bad; this is not our present affair. They are there!

While remembering that the larger framework of western civilization was moulded within the Christian consciousness, we may not forget that men belong to civil communities, possess property, enjoy protection from injury, in a word, are legal persons. Limits of space preclude adequate discussion of Roman law in this connection. Suffice it to point out that this, the greatest gift of Rome to posterity, could not have developed as it

did without the interposition of Stoicism. For
centuries prior to her effective contact with
Greek modes of thought, Rome observed her
own law, the civil law (law of the city) or, in
the expression which indicates its *local* character, the law of the *Quirites* — of those who
shared full rights of citizenship. As conquest
brought expansion and constant intercourse
with subject allies, putative enemies, and
'barbarians' (earlier law differentiated sharply
between the three classes), another type of
law gained recognition slowly. This was the
Jus Gentium, not our modern "law of nations," but usages so observed by aliens as to
have the effect of law among them. Another
and, probably, later name for the new departure seems to have been *Jus Commune,* a norm
acknowledged by both parties to a cause almost
as matter of 'common sense,' and therefore
usual in that it might be anticipated among
'decent' people. It embodied 'immemorial
usage,' not technical or statuted legality which
might well drift far from equity. But it did
not revert to metaphysical principles. Thus
another step had to be taken: hence, whatever the origin of the *Jus Gentium* at Rome
(still in doubt), it came to be regarded, not

as a code drawn in the special interest of aliens, nor even as a selection from their ways, but simply as the body of universal principles 'naturally' presupposed by all particular or municipal laws. This transition was mediated by Cicero and by the great jurisconsults of the Empire who, like directing Romans then, professed Stoicism almost as a religion. It would be a misapprehension to infer that Stoicism dominated specific statutes. In this respect it was like Christianity in Europe later, or the Utilitarian philosophy in liberal England after 1832. It furnished a certain ideal which, operating over a long period, transformed the *Jus Gentium*, an *exception*, into a rational system so flexible and sane as to become the embodiment of equity for western society.

We have seen that the Greeks were agitating high questions about Law and Justice and Right at a time when Rome was little more than a rural village. They were learning that Rights pertain to persons, operate between persons, and that the community would consult its own safety did it abstain from constant meddling with these " faculties." Moreover, they were seeing dimly what the Romans never saw at all, that there may be Rights, pertain-

ing to immaterial or spiritual affairs of human
nature, of such intense significance as to merit
the description " absolute." This reached beyond the most generous Roman interpretation
of the *Jus Gentium* or *Jus Commune,* which
predicated observances already current. You
may term the further step abstraction, if you
please. It involved the typical Stoic notion
of a " partnership of mankind " inseparable
from the order of the universe. As such, it
may consort with the *Jus Gentium.* Even so, it
portends a transcendental ideal, that is, a state
of relations not yet realized, but eminently to
be desired. The Stoics called it *Jus Naturale,*
nigh a divine law, assuredly the origin, likewise
the final cause, of all law. In other words,
they supplied the sole philosophical ideas in
which the Romans proved quite at home, —
the speculative basis for systematic thought
about Law and Justice and Rights. More important, they loosed the impulse whereby
changes might be made in the temper of legal
institutions. Briefly, the *Jus Naturale* injected
a socio-political factor into the calculations of
jurists which was destined to be of immeasur-
able influence later throughout western history.
Jumping the centuries, contemporary " unrest "

seems to testify to its potency now; and, if we consider all the implications of the Virginia " Declaration of Rights," of the " Declaration of Independence," and of the Constitution, we hardly exaggerate in suggesting that, without " the politics of a higher region " incident to the Stoic Law of Nature, the independent commonwealth known as the United States of America would never have found *reason* for existence.

As concerns the larger framework, then, our debt to Stoicism needs no emphasizing, once we recall it.

2. WITHIN THE CULTURE OF LATIN CHRISTIANITY

After the Augustinian epoch the cosmological or Greek factor in eclectic Stoicism recedes, because speculation has projected a world where man can be at home. Theology transcends metaphysics; the qualities of the universe, from Stoic order to Platonic love, become divine Attributes. Fate is transmuted into Providence manifesting the Plan of Salvation. Men *in puris naturalibus* are supported by prevenient Grace. In the same way,

the ascetic tendency of Roman moralist Stoicism is masked by the practical interest of
Christianity, and by approval of the monastic
life. Further, the substitution of Latin for
Greek as the language of the Church and of the
learned, favours a tradition whereby the naturalism of the Stoics is displaced by mystic
survivals of Plato or Neoplatonism in Augustine. Then, too, the disturbances wrought by
the westerly migrations of the tribes, by the
consequent readjustments in secular affairs
and, in another way, by the appearance of
dialects, led to intellectual atrophy which
reached its depths about the middle of the
ninth century, when even Latin was in par-
lous case.[30] Indeed, till the eleventh century,
this maxim sufficed:

Scire Deus satis est, quo nulla scientia major.

Nevertheless, thanks mainly to the authority
of Cicero, Virgil, and Seneca, and to the Stoic
loans in eclectic Platonism, occasional reminis-
cences may be detected.

Macrobius (c. 400–430), whom Neoplatonism claims, uses Stoic material. In the
Saturnalia he adopts Seneca's humanitarianism toward slaves; his treatment of the pagan

[133]

gods, and the interpretation of *anima* presup-
pose the Stoic cosmology; and he thinks of
philosophy as essential to *virtue*. Accordingly,
his Commentary on the *Somnium Scipionis* of
Cicero, although deflected by Neopythagoreanism, presents the Stoic doctrine of the hegemony of Reason in the individual soul and,
reckoning with the dogma of a world-conflagra-
tion in such a way as to prefigure Neo-Stoicism
in our own day, he reverts to the view that
" virtue " is sufficient for happiness, temporal
or eternal. The dutiful (*pius*) spirit of this
commentary attested the persistence of the
unction peculiar to Roman Stoicism, and thus
exerted influence later in approving Cicero to
Christian believers.

Again, take Boëthius (*c.* 470–524), " the last
of the Romans whom Cato or Tully could have
acknowledged for their countryman," as Gibbon has it. Certainly not Cato, Tully perhaps!
For, his Neoplatonism is obvious, as his psychology shows emphatically, and yet, his
attitude to Fate, Fortune, and Providence and,
more clearly, his notion of rewards and pun-
ishments, are inconceivable without Stoicism.
He knew Cicero and Seneca intimately, and he
clung to pre-Christian ideology, applying it

to Christian problems, however. He believes that men may reach perfection ' naturally,' that is, without the operation of divine Grace. For, spurning the things of this world and, supported by philosophy, they can attain the Highest Good. Stoic imperturbability is set forth in the *Consolation of Philosophy*. Hence, the emphasis upon the uncertainty of mundane happiness, to say nothing of the information about Aristotle, Porphyry, and ' universals,' gave Boëthius magistral vogue during the Middle Ages. He preserved the ethically rational, having no inclination to declare, *Mea grammatica Christus est*. This awaited the kind of outlook possible to a Peter Damianus at the end of the " dark " Ages.

Traces of Stoicism fade now for centuries, till, indeed, men regained Latin and, divining the ancient spirit in their manner, — paganism esteemed the *praecursor Christi in naturalibus,* — were emboldened to " remember a moral found in a tale," as Gerbert (Pope, 999–1003) put it. John of Salisbury, Bernard Silvestris, Peter of Blois, William of Conches, above all, Hildebert (1055–1123) represent this literary-reflective mood. The last, an urbane wit, is a forerunner of the Renaissance: loving an-

cient letters and the wisdom thereof; culling
beauty of conduct from philosophical knowledge, to adopt his own phrase; sure that the
' natural ' man, fortified by the pathos of Virgil, and the " virtue " of Persius, Cicero, Seneca, and Quintilian, nay, liberated by the play-
fulness of Ovid, knows where to find suffic-
ing consolations.[31]

Thereafter, despite the Stoicism of the
Philosopher in Abelard's *Dialogus inter philos-
ophum, Judaeum, et Christianum,* and the ex-
hibition of Stoic inwardness in his doctrine
of conscience (*scito te ipsum*), we must not
expect to find the individualistic schools in-
fluencing the philosophical developments of the
thirteenth century. The platonizing Stoicism
of Augustine gives way to matters of immediate
concern — the Arabians, and the ' new ' Aristotle. Of course, Stoic fragments are there, as
of Galen in Albert the Great, but they effect
little or nothing. Roger Bacon, Duns Scotus,
and Occam (1300–47) had other fish to fry.
As with Dante, the Stoics are *in* the Elysian
Fields, not *of* the vital moment.

Lecky writes: " In no respect is the greatness of the Stoic philosophers more conspicuous than in the contrast between the gigantic

steps of legal reform made in a few years
under their influence, and the almost insignifi-
cant steps taken when Christianity had obtained an ascendancy in the empire, not to
speak of the long period of decrepitude that
followed." [32] However this may be, one must
remember that, when the first onset of the
Renaissance (*c.* 1050–1350) manifested itself,
at Pavia, Ravenna, and Bologna, in renewed
study of Roman law, Stoic principles were read
in the light of Christian problems, theological
and political. The ' natural law ' of the equality and fraternity of mankind is there, but
touched to fresh issues. The protest of St.
Bernard intimates no less: *Quidem quotidie
perstrepunt in palatio leges, sed Justiniani,
non Domini.* Canon law and Christian modes
of thought, not to speak of theological conclusions, had shifted the point of reference. It
is true that the Stoic *Jus Naturale* continues
a principle of benignity justifying the description of law as *ars boni et aequi:* but preoc-
cupation with its divine relations or with its
import for ecclesiastico-political arrangements
had supervened upon its guarantee of consider-
ate justice to individuals. Necessarily, first-
hand investigation uncovered Stoic ideas;

[137]

as necessarily, the *Jus Naturale,* having been read into the " Gospel," took on specific divine sanction — *divine leges natura consistent.* In short, a movement has started bound to gravitate toward the *dictum* of Suarez (1568–1619), *Lex injusta non est lex.* With this, a door is opened wide to political casuistry. ' Natural law ' takes rank — almost precedence — as an *a priori* source, warranting contrary interpretations of disputable cases. In point of fact, a tendency ensued to erect two abstractions: on the one hand, a *Jus Naturale* or *Lex Naturalis* whereby men share in the moral order of the universe deducible by unaided ' natural reason ': on the other, a *Jus Divinum,* revealed to humanity with supernatural intent, to wit, the preservation of the *absolutely* valuable single soul to immortal life. When the former is subordinated to the latter, and by an authoritative organization, all may go well. But, when Cynic rationalism, guiltless of revealed sanctions, returns to magnify the former, the ' unwritten ' law may justify any abrogations and in any interest. " Universal consent is the voice of nature," as Cicero said; but, consent about what? Allow an ideal of excellence to penetrate practical politics, and you have adopted an ethical conception in semi-legal guise which may lead very far afield. Thus, going behind the attitude of the Roman jurisconsults, the legal renaissance of the eleventh century hinted the possibility of a code superior to, and therefore capable of abrogating, man-made laws. So long as " divine law " interpreted by the Church Universal remained powerful, tangential novelties were stayed. But, with the disintegration accompanying the Renaissance and Reformation, the Stoic doctrine might presage anything, from ' national ' rights to counsels of political despair. The ' modern ' world was to furnish many examples.

3. THE GREAT TRANSITION [33]

The streams of obscene or wearisome Billingsgate catapulted so impartially upon each other by the half-laics of the Renaissance and the whole-clerics of the Reformation might well justify the suspicion that passions had been aroused, or that contemporary disputes had been magnified, to such a degree as to preclude all clear, not to say circumspect, thought. To a certain extent this is true. In any case,

the period marks a transition when ideas
hitherto mutually tolerant fell apart, inviting
experimental combinations, or adjustment to a
fresh perspective. Thanks to its cosmology
on the one hand, to its moral teaching on the
other, Stoicism revived in the general stimulus.
Naturally, the inimical schools of Scepticism
and Epicureanism raised their heads again.
But, lacking a tradition of authoritative names
from of old and, more fatal, popular literary
sources, their recovery forms no more than an
incident. On the contrary, Stoicism of a kind
becomes so ubiquitous that its case invites
overstatement. It looms through the dissolv-
ing haze.

Despite the prodigalities of the bubbling
ferment, a broad situation can be detected.
The Middle Ages being in bankruptcy, with
Italy " the corruption of the world," the intellectual and moral virtues essential to recon-
struction have no existence. Appeal is taken
silently to the mighty Past, the Past of Italic
memory, but the knowledge of Greek, requisite to successful enlistment of ancient thought,
lags. On the other hand, the naturalization
of Latin literature, and the anaesthetizing of
virtue at its sources, gave Stoicism an obvious

advantage. But, allowing this, the movement passed over the heads of the ' common people,' who were not to be drawn into it ere the Reformation. Hence, negations tended to outrun affirmations, no system being vigorous enough to produce originative minds capable of thoroughgoing constructions. Hellenistic syncretism, or fusion of doctrines drawn from various, sometimes incompatible, sources, was not understood by Renaissance scholars. We know now that Cicero, who professed himself a follower of the Academic Sceptics, went over to Stoicism at last; that Horace, usually classed with the Epicureans, touched his wise acquiescences with Stoic ideas; that Virgil had profound Stoic affinities which poetic insight enabled him to illuminate; and that Seneca, notwithstanding his Stoicism, held Epicurus in high esteem. Now, these are precisely the most influential Latins during this period.[34] It is not wonderful, then, that even when other sects seem to claim some Renaissance men, Stoic moralism, especially in its pathetic rejection of life or in its more pathetic ' return to nature,' should fascinate. This is true of so-called ' Ciceronians ' like Rudolph Agricola and Vives, who hold that ethics is the vital part of philosophy, and recommend 'experimental' study of conduct; true of the Sceptical group, from Rabelais through Montaigne to Charron; while even the Epicurean, Gassendi, adopts the Stoic wise man as his ideal — the man who is saved from Fate to find freedom under the law of virtue for its own sake.

Nothing could be more symptomatic than the dialogue *De Voluptate* (*c.* 1440) of L. Valla. We see mediæval ethics in the melting-pot. Valla concerns himself with man in this life, not with preparation of the soul for a life to come. Epicureanism as an Italian Humanist understood it was brought into the lists against Stoic morality read in the light of Christian asceticism. The contrasts are drawn admirably, with a tenderness for the Epicurean side. Thus, though Valla adjudges the Stoic to have the better of it, he flogs monachism, and makes it plain that "a life according to nature" is, after all, practicable and superior. The arguments interest us little now; the point to note is that the unquestioned authority of ecclesiastical standards is broken and, heaven being ruled out, the assize sits on earth. A decade later the German mind, surer in grasp

and searching deeper, finds expression in the
Idiota of Nicolas of Cusa, where the Stoic cosmology, with its immanent deity, is substituted
for the dualist transcendence orthodox among
Scholastics. But, on the whole, Italians com-
mand the movement. Pomponazzi (1462–
1524), and the Calabrians (*c.* 1565–1639),
Telesius, Campanella, and Bruno, mediate the
transition.

Four phases are discernible, intertwined as
a rule. First, there is a reaction, seldom running the length of complete revolt, against
ecclesiastical authority in thought and asceticism in life. Second, the curiosity and human-
ism of the ancients fill the gap, with some
bias against Aristotle, however; he had come
to serve the enemy. Third, a new object of
study looms up. A positive return to nature
must be made, by way of observation and
experiment, or by reference to the sensuous
side of individual experience, which seems to
imply personal freedom operating within a
causal series. The Stoic doctrine of self-gov-
ernment (*principale* of Seneca) finds a niche
here, and points to a *lay* morality. Fourth,
and incidentally at first, serious effort is made
to link these views with Christian doctrine and

the interests of the Church, in short, to show
that acceptable belief receives just as effective,
and much more reasonable, support from the
new as from the old methods. On the whole,
it may be said that the movement turns its
face from ' other-worldliness ' to ' this-world-
liness,' Stoic cosmology assisting, and that, in
the final issue, adjustment to Christian doctrine
becomes the dominating motive, Stoic moralism, a kind of Proteus, assuming unforeseen
rôles in evangelical theology and utilitarian
nationalist politics.

Pomponazzi,[35] intent upon reinterpretation
of Aristotle, concentrated upon metaphysical
and psychological rather than ethical problems.
The relation between ' mind ' and ' matter,'
the immortality of the soul, and the bearing
of Providence upon individual liberty enthrall
him. Hence Stoicism is quite subordinate,
though never forgotten. Following Alexander
of Aphrodisias and, probably, Macrobius, Pomponazzi denies the subsistence of mind in
matter. But, being a consistent empiricist, he
conceives nature as a *datum* whence alone
valid inferences can be drawn. This means
abandonment of personal immortality and, of
course, of the chief moral sanction. Thrown

upon his own ' natural ' resources, man thus
reverts to the *homo temperatus* of Stoicism,
the moral law becomes *qui proprie hominis est*
— a forecast of Kantian universalist rigorism.
A ' morality without religion ' or, at least, without revelation, suffices. Inevitably, too, in
his treatment of free-will, destiny, and providence, Pomponazzi trades upon the capital
bequeathed by Stoicism. He preserves astrology, Stoic or other, turning it to excellent
critical account against magic and superstition — " wrong in his facts, but right in his
method of reasoning." Despite his persistent
naturalism, he professes himself a thorough
conformist in matters not amenable to reason.

It is possible that the Stoic doctrine of a
world-soul, restated by the physician-mathema-
tician, Cardanus (*c.* 1552), may have affected
Telesius. Be this as it may, they agree that
natural causes governed by natural laws permeate the universe, and that philosophy must
traffic with these. But, while Cardanus is
insistent upon the authority of the Church,
Telesius' eleventh-hour recantation leaves it
quite apparent that he divorced philosophy
entirely from theological dogma. It is a secular pursuit pure and simple. Accordingly, he

holds the soul to be " a very subtile essence,"
a Stoic reminiscence. But he thinks forward,
not back, and his substitution of ' natural
philosophy ' for metaphysics hints his real
significance. Campanella leaves an uncertain
impression in much the same way. For, although he held sense-perception to be the basis
of all knowledge, he also thought, like the
Stoics, that every man ' harbours a spark of the
divine,' which guarantees intellectual certainty.
Apparently, he was unaware of the scepticism
inseparable from this position. In his social
philosophy he assumed the Stoic unity of mankind, and yet made equalitarianism the ground
for an aristocratic state. Bruno, the boldest
mind of the group, was endowed with poetic
imagination, Cleanthes his spiritual prototype.
Outreaching the movement, he pointed to
something beyond — before due time. In his
early work, he employs the world-soul, part of
stock-in-trade Stoic hylozoism. Later, he
forecasts a philosophy which would reckon
mind a developing force in history. While this
preserves remnants of Stoicism, they are em-
bedded in a theory foreign to Hellenic thought.
Thus, his Heraclitus is hardly Heraclitus as
we understand him now; his final pantheism

differs widely from hylozoism. The tendency is prophetic of impending change. Stoic views continue to survive, but rather as moods accompanying the adoption of the Copernican theory on the one hand, or the interests awakened by the Reformation on the other.

This is illustrated aptly by the fate which overtook the single conscious revival of Stoicism in the period.[36] Caspar Schoppe (Scioppius, c. 1606) has left scarce a rack behind. Justus Lipsius (Jost Lips, c. 1593) hardly merited Mark Pattison's jibe, "the narrow pedant." Yet, his simplicity of character, attested by tell-tale devotion to an idealized Seneca, and his pure affection for learning, while they keep his memory green, particularly at Louvain, could not breathe life into his philosophy. A generous feeling after *recta ratio* did not suffice to redeem an isolated position, and it was by accident of circumstance rather than by native insight that he fought a rearguard action for that predilection in favour of Stoicism as against Neoplatonizing incomprehensibles, quite traceable in the Humanist succession. And why? Lipsius might have declared with perfect sincerity, and with Montaigne, " the use to which I put my studies is a practical one — the formation of character for the exigencies of life." No bespattered *Athanasius contra mundum*, like his Basel contemporary, Taurellus, he was in and of the same world.

The formation of the dogmatics of evangelical Protestantism, now well along, had effectually foreclosed a "sound learning" which, as Erasmus wrote to Maldonato two generations earlier, would nobly "celebrate Christ, in whom we ought to boast as the sole author of both wisdom and happiness if we are true Christians." For, if Greece rose from the dead in the Renaissance, it was "with the New Testament in her hand." "Rest not in an ovation, but a triumph over thy passions." This, and much other advice given by Sir Thomas Browne in the *Letter to a Friend*,[37] catches the accent of Stoicism. But when, reading on, we find, "He who thus ordereth the purpose of this life will never be far from the next," we realize that Christian morals are in mind also. Nor in the realm of knowledge was it otherwise. In five stanzas of "Nosce Teipsum" (1599), Sir John Davies gives a remarkable transcript of the Stoic "union" between body and soul, but passes from the

'elegy' on human learning to the 'elegy' on
the immortality of the soul.

The practical causes of the Reformation
were doubtless complex, and opinions may continue to differ about the respective importance
of the social, ecclesiastical, economic, and
political factors.[38] The theoretical point of
departure is by no means so obscure. For,
although philosophy underwent temporary
eclipse, the very intolerance of the sixteenth
and seventeenth centuries served to define the
broad issue and, at the same time, rendered
'common men' partizans of ideas. Discus-
sions maintained by a select few during the
Renaissance passed to wider circles. Hence,
partly through heat of passion; partly through
ignorance of classical literature; most of all
thanks to a historical situation, the outgrowth
of centuries, which formulated the chief question in one way rather than another, *direct*
touch with Græco-Roman concepts was lost
by many. The Stoic contribution hung over,
so to speak, but absorbed in such a manner
that its formative power went unheeded. It
reappeared ere long in technical philosophy.
" Descartes was really a Stoic in his ethical

attitude; so were Spinoza, Leibnitz, and others." [39] Feudalism, church polity, and the 'conflict between Pope and Emperor' intervened meanwhile to deflect.

For example, throughout the development of the Papacy and of feudal authoritarianism, nothing is more remarkable than the unbroken continuity of Græco-Roman speculative ideas.[40] Epicurean, Sceptic and, notably, Stoic positions recur. Like Carneades and the Sceptics, Machiavelli denies a *jus naturale*, deeming Justice no more than a convention. The Epicurean view, that individual self-sufficiency renders the State superfluous, had its proponents; so, too, the Stoic doctrine, that this identical self-sufficiency serves the State and, even more characteristic, that study avails to goodness. Similarly, there are ways in which Posidonius and Seneca appear 'modern'; they believe in a primitive condition of human innocence, and thus provide basis for the suggestion of Rufinus (*c.* 400), that the State was conceived in iniquity, born in sin. This variation of the 'baleful Nimroud' legend was destined to originate many disturbances later.

Moreover, it is obvious that the emphasis placed on personality by Seneca indicates his advance beyond Plato and Aristotle, and implies the possibility of an individual relationship with God. This notion was reborn at the dawn of the Reformation as *The Obedience of a Christian Man* (1528). Here, then, is the root of the theory of " germinal holiness," a matter of controversy among the Reformers; an aspect of the Counter-Reformation, especially in Jesuit teaching; thereafter favouring the idea that man is potentially omniscient and, finally, eliciting the influential pronouncement of Kant.[41] During this lengthy interval, it was fated to induce all sorts of vagaries about ' liberty.' For instance, after the original appeal to the downtrodden, Christianity became a prop of empire, only to create a hierarchy which thrust itself into the breach against feudal tyrannies with the doctrine of a ' natural ' law that is ' divine,' thus restoring the lost theory of the ultimate authority of the Roman *people,* and spreading it abroad over Europe. Already in the far north at the beginning of the fourteenth century (1320), the Scots, speaking through the Parliament of Arbroath for their excommunicated king, Robert the Bruce, and addressing Pope John XXII, declare: " We care not for glory or for wealth,

[151]

but for that liberty which no true man will give up but with his life." To the same effect, supporting the Papacy now, Aquinas wrote; " All real authority is derived from popular suffrage, and all laws must be made by the people or their representatives." While Marsilius of Padua,[42] attacking the pretensions of the Papacy, lays down the same principle. " Laws derive their authority from the nation, and are invalid without its assent. . . . As men are equal, it is wrong that one should be bound by laws made by another. . . . But in obeying laws to which all have agreed, all men, in reality, govern themselves." We are not far, here, from the theoretical *crux* of the Reformation — Justification by Faith. As Luther put it: " A good tree brings forth good fruit by nature, without compulsion; is it not madness to prescribe laws to an apple-tree that it should bear apples and not thorns? " But, thanks to vital interests down the centuries, the moralism connected with Grace covered the traces of its Stoic parentage. Nevertheless, the substance of the old teaching remains, incidental if you will, never expelled altogether. Luther went to St. Paul for his proofs of Justification by Faith, leaving his successors to wrestle with

the problems raised by Pelagius (Cicero, Seneca) in relation to the interpretation of the
Augustinian reply. Calvin reckoned with
Seneca at the outset, only to deny him, and
then to adopt something curiously akin to Stoic
cosmology in his ' supralapsarian ' universe
which, however, proved too ' high ' for softer
folk, unable to inure themselves to " the
spiritual city built upon Stoicism on the rock
of predestination." Zwingli timidly, Melancthon definitely, made concession to free activity
of the will and to ' natural ' righteousness, the
facultas sese applicandi ad gratiam being reminiscent of such admirations as extorted Augustine's comment on Seneca: " What more
could a Christian say than this Pagan has
said? " At length, human experience, self-
torturing yet self-sustaining, faces the irreconcilable facts and, content but unjoyous, speaks
forthright in Pascal, the Christian Marcus
Aurelius who, thanks to his ascetic theology,
finds " principles of diabolical pride " in the
Stoics. With English genius for compromise,
Bishop Butler could pocket the pride. " The
very constitution of our nature requires that we
bring our whole conduct before this superior
faculty [conscience]; wait its determination;

[153]

enforce upon ourselves its authority, and make it the business of our lives, as it is absolutely the whole business of a moral agent, to conform ourselves to it." This is pure Stoicism — almost. Christian experience suggests something else. We must deal with impulses as ' natural,' and set them on the way they should go. We must not dismiss inequalities and other evils as unreal, but find them incitements to an ideal justice. Hence, Butler had many disciples, some unfaithful and peculiar enough; Pascal stood aloof. In the one, Stoicism proved ductile, in the other, it withdrew.

The Reformation embodied a protest against the moral licence and intellectual pride of the Renaissance. It invoked free ethical personality acting from the necessity of the Divine nature. But awesome conviction of supernatural duty did not rid it of a human nature ' fully persuaded in its own mind.' Hence, all unwitting, it lent further impulse to a secularizing process which could not avoid drafts upon ancient wisdom; affinity bridged the immense gulf of circumstance. Inconvenient questions about the relation between king and people, State and Church, emerged with the growth of

nationalism. Consequently, the Italian ' tyran-
nicide,' who lost Christ through admiration
for Brutus, found many imitators apt to learn
Knox's admonition to Queen Mary: " If
princes exceed their bounds . . . to bind their
hands is no disobedience . . . but just obedience, because it agreeth with the Word of God."
So, over a long period, apotheosis of the Stoic
' opposition,' and parade of Cæsar as the incarnation of evil by closet-republicans like
William Godwin (1793), are signs of the times,
the more significant the less the historical
knowledge of hero or reprobate! As for Cicero, who wrote of Brutus, " I have lost . . . a
comrade and associate in *high endeavour*," the
very wealth of his remains made him a genius
or a thing of shreds and patches, from Persius
and Jerome to Middleton (1741) and Mommsen. In a word, the Stoic missionary to reason
and conscience had revealed *universal traits,
manifest in every civilized society.*

These intangible forces, deprived of age-old
sanctions and confronted with novel situations,
bade men seek certainty. English Deism,
led by Locke and Newton; Dutch Criticism
and French *Spiritisme,* thinking in terms of
Descartes, the Cartesians, and Spinoza; Teu-

tonic Illumination, inchoate in Leibnitz, majestic in Kant; and Gallic Scepticism, legatee of Montaigne, the *pensées* writers, and Bayle, arose to smoothe or intensify the difficulties. All were intellectual or voluntaristic, reposing confidence precisely in abstract reason or inward conscience, and therefore, like the Stoics, devoid of historic sense. The mild or militant rationalism which rendered them ' modern ' had, nevertheless, subtle affinities with Greek naturalism, or Roman humanitarianism and self-sufficiency. Spinoza apart, loose metaphysics gained vogue, and loose metaphysics seem inseparable from cynicism in ethics, irresponsibility in political action. Consequently, the Divine Right of Kings — Cæsarism mediated through Machiavelli and Luther — was invoked to redress the balance.[43] When, thanks to national exigencies, this took rank as a ' fundamental law of nature,' harried minorities or dissident *blocs* cast themselves upon a speculative liberalism, enheartened by the example of the ' great liberators ' of the past, always justified by ' reason and conscience.' Stoic equalitarianism, answering to a new mood in a new Silver Age, entered the latest generalization and, itself unknown, was known by all!

No accident led a great publishing house to begin its career with *Seneca's Morals* (Harper Brothers, 1817); from Oxford to Dartmouth, undergraduates were discussing " Cicero as a Statesman," " The Communism of the Munster Anabaptists," " Aspirants for Civil and Religious Liberty," and so forth. Humanitarianism, democracy, individualism, philanthropy, perfectibility, natural equality — a recondite jumble of human and divine imponderables — were the current shibboleths. Having proven Fate irrational in its dealings with them, men fell back upon their own resources content, for the rest, with a respectful gesture to a remote deity. But general ideas betoken a philosophy, bound to disturb although outside the immediate practical programme of the Reformers. So, ' natural law,' ' natural right,' ' natural equality,' ' natural goodness,' above all, ' natural theology,' gathered themselves together in Natural Religion. Grotius, a persuasive ethical rather than a didactic intellectual force; Hooker, deeming that " nature hath use " as much as " need for grace," and that " the light of nature . . . reason, is from God;" Locke, tolerant to a fault, because the " foundation of all virtue is . . . placed in this, that a man is able to

[157]

deny himself his own desires . . . and purely follow what reason directs as best," started a movement which, thanks to combination of ' common sense ' incoherence with Stoic sincerity, can still beset public opinion. For, the quasi-legal ethics of Cicero and other eclectics, and the Roman law of nature, seen through the divine law of the Decalogue, might well justify discontent and, better still, furnish it an appellate tribunal, provided a *Weltanschauung* were forthcoming. And come it did — a theory of ' natural liberty,' saturated with optimism; of eternal divine decrees, fatalistic logically, but to be borne practically, because they freed each man from all others. This philosophy of the inviolable single citizen (so one might term it) could not but recognize its own image and superscription in " guidance derived by natural insight from natural principles." On the ethical side, Shaftesbury's " autonomy of the moral element;" on the cosmological, Toland's activist materialism, or Diderot's hylozoism, — " the whole of matter is filled with activity and sensibility," — tell why. It would be fruitless to claim that a Natural Religion which, objectively, " consists in the natural moral law," subjectively " in the submission to it that is

founded on conviction," reproduced Stoicism
closely. It would be equally fruitless to repudi-
ate affinities. There is the same attempt to
render a forbidding universe friendly; there is
the same tonic morality governed by conscience sure of itself; there is an ideal of human brotherhood, hitched to another star —
still, a star. Nay, the final implication betrays
similarity. Man must return upon self ultimately, because even ethics " has no imperative or constructive character, but is entirely
descriptive." As in much else, Hume was to
make this plain, unveiling our ' modern '
subjectivity, devoid of Greek ingenuousness
and Roman self-command, but a prey to the
recurrent nostalgia for harmonious unity.

4. The Nineteenth Century

Seeing we must anticipate resemblance of
mood or outlook rather than discipleship to a
system, it is well to recall that Stoicism faces
three ways. When the Greeks began to doubt
the old gods, thinkers, Plato conspicuously, ex-
plained the world in terms of idealistic pantheism. The Stoics adhered to the same view sub-
stantially. They detected a universal reason

permeating all things; over against this they set
'matter;' but they evaded antagonism by
holding that reason was itself material and, because good, the governor of 'matter.' Hence
their doctrine of a 'world-soul.' In ethics, they
set pursuit of the ideal above pleasure, insistent that the freedom of the rational soul in
thought, manifesting itself in effort to produce
a type of character, *ought* to rule life. Third,
this moral energism was sanctioned by a 'natural' law superior in authority to convention
and, consequently, the guarantee of certain inviolable rights. Characteristic estimates of the
world and of the *common* man resulted, readily
adjustable to knowledge, morals, and politics.
Indeed, the flexibility, not the harmony, of
the ideas lent them persistent influence. While,
then, there is little or no conscious recurrence
to them during the nineteenth century, parallel cases emerge, largely because human nature does not change. There are roseate hopes
for the future, sublime conviction in the present, lambent appeals to the past, with attendant
doubts no less moving. And, once aspiration
or protest has been aroused, any man, particularly any 'great' man, may be anarchical, —
" a little one shall become a thousand, and a

small one a strong nation." Moreover, Christianity offers an allied message. *Non est corpus tam vile pro quo mortuus est Christus.* Stoicism conserved the tone calculated to freight many such issues with *immediate* seriousness.

Returning, then, recollect that Hume did not intrude his antiseptic scepticism upon the affairs of the work-a-day world. His " Stoic " assumes principles shamelessly.[44] Nature has " endowed " man " with a sublime celestial spirit. . . . Acknowledge, therefore, O man, the beneficence of nature; for she has given thee that intelligence which supplies all thy necessities." Though unable to go so far as his younger contemporary, Adam Smith, Hume shares the optimism of the age, taking no thought of *Candide* (1759). This temper survived for a season. Inspired by it, Condorcet (1794) could dream of " mankind marching with a firm step along the road of truth, virtue, and happiness." Indeed, he set no limit to hope. The farther removed the future golden age, the more seductive it grew, as we notice in Shelley later. For, the *philosophes,* ridden by several fanaticisms, professed a general optimism, condemning particulars the while. They could affirm with Cicero's Stoic: *magna*

[161]

di curant, parva neglegunt. But the Revolution, Napoleon, and Reaction were to sweep Europe, leaving disillusion in their wake. 'Liberty' was to simmer down to letting all "make their own bargains;" 'Equality' to "bettering this wicked world by covering it with Republics," as Bentham advised (1824); 'Fraternity' to the Australian ballot. The inflated balloons, sagging, came down to earth as 'representative government' on the Austinian plan — "perception of utility." What a falling off! Natural rights, "nonsense upon stilts"! A generous democratic eclecticism, Stoic in its Puritan survivals, might be one result. We see it in John Stuart Mill, whose theological troubles reproduce Seneca.[45] Another might be despair of the ideal, arising from conviction that the 'inner law,' because opposed by the cruel world, could never induce order there. We see it in Henri Frédéric Amiel, a timid Stoic, whose *l'abandon à Dieu* evaporates into thin air, reason and conscience enfeebled by mutual antagonism.[46] But, between the Utilitarian adjustment, which presupposed a quasi-Epicurean creed, and the *défiance* with *impuissance,* which afflict one phase of Stoicism, other outlets appeared. The material is so vast, so complex, and so near withal, that nothing more than a few notes can be attempted. Further, they must be at random more or less, for everyone would make his own selection.

In a general way, the wealth of moral observation accumulated during the first half of the nineteenth century is traceable to the Romantic movement. And, if Romanticism be the retreat of reason before feeling and imagination, we should not expect Stoic moods. They insinuate themselves nevertheless. Herder's cosmopolitanism did much to detach Goethe from Gallic turbulence. It affected his latent Epicureanism also, giving him a vision of the 'archical man,' the man who can rule. But Goethe could not rise to the occasion, opportunity withholding the unconscious wholeness of the Greek, and the severity in grapple of the Roman. A pre-revolution mind, he could not have caught the full import of Victor Hugo's post-revolution apostrophe: "Science is beautiful, Aristotle great, but Socrates and Zeno greater still!" Although he could be brought to cry, "Soul of the world, come and permeate us," his peculiar 'return to nature' was too amoral for Stoicism. He never asked Fichte's question: " How can moral order and political freedom be made to agree? " Accordingly, he had scant sympathy with Schiller's semi-Stoic reply: " To be a moral being is man's destiny. Virtue, not virtues, is his task; and virtue is nothing but an instinct for duty." Schiller's fusion of Platonic warmth with Stoic rigour testified to the stress which elicited Fichte's doctrine, that man must become free by conscious effort. No doubt, this self-reliance took service under the banner of that new idea, the Time-Spirit, and implied devotion to a ' cause.' As Hegel was to show, it involved the notion of that ' larger whole,' the State, and thus went behind the conditions productive of Stoicism. Still, it signalled a battle " not for human rights, but for the divine rights of man." In other words, man is able to help himself on his own resources, nay, to help deity, as Carlyle put it. There *is* a ' natural ' freedom, and eventual judgment will run according to the use made of it.

This conception, essentially Stoic, winds like a scarlet thread through the fabric of German poetry and theology.[47] If not in the individual, then in *his* group, freedom pulsates to mighty ends. Indeed, Stoicism, mediated through Pelagianism, reappears constantly in liberal Protestantism, sometimes with most curious, not to say startling, effects. On the other hand, in France, where the theological question remained subordinate, and æsthetic squabbles kept Romanticism esoteric, it is the politicians and social visionaries — Enfantin, Comte, Quinet, for instance — who betray similar leanings,

" *Bellowing victory, bellowing doom.*"

Again, the spiritual experience of the English-speaking world took another path. Political experiment, territorial expansion, and industrial activity, appearing to be successful, held the foreground for a time. Voices reckoned great now were crying in the wilderness then, preaching to a stiff-necked generation. Wordsworth, Shelley, Carlyle, Emerson, Thoreau, Ruskin had their day of " most unqualified disapprobation." Thoreau aside (he was of the Cynic sect), all might be called Platonists. But, as they unfold their tale, we find Platonism own cousin to Stoicism. Take Wordsworth. His ' Stoicism,' as in the " Ode to Duty," has become a commonplace. One would rather emphasize his art. His best poetry reinterpreted Nature, transmuting her prosaic " air, earth, and skies " into " Powers that will work for thee;" finding guarantee of " man's unconquerable mind " in " something far more deeply interfused," whereby

> " we taste
> The pleasure of believing what we see
> Is boundless, as we wish our souls to be."

His " attempt to breathe grandeur upon the very humblest form of human life " is plain Stoicism — Christianized or, rather, Puritanized. Again, take the Scots Confucius. He was a good deal of a Cynic, — *ipse mihi theatrum,* — with an " Old-Roman contempt of the superfluous," adjudging Byron " a dandy of sorrows . . . a sham strong man." Yet this was but one soul-side. Commerce with Epictetus, with the early Fichte and, in all probability, a Berkeleyan cosmology, evoked the other. " God is round us and in us, Here as well as Yonder;" man is " the Announcer of himself and of his Freedom." Accordingly, the greatest passage in the greatest chapter of his greatest book, where he forthtells that we " are, in very deed, Ghosts," is pure Stoicism.[48] Kindred ideas reverberate antiphonally among the idealists of the flowering time. Nor are realists wanting, to vent moods redolent of Stoic moralism. Taking no account of the novels, it is sufficient to select " The Old Stoic " from the verses of the Brontë sisters in order to find solemn fearlessness confronting the inscrutable.

After 1850, romanticists and systematists tiring, changes make themselves felt. Remarkable acquisitions in every science, from physics to philology, unsettle old sanctions, and the prentice hand is tried upon substitutes. " Dynamics and Prose Composition have met together; Literature and Biology have kissed each other." The dawn of Cosmic Emotion comes up. Minds of the most varied hue, of the most contrasted background, gravitate towards a conception of ' divine Nature ' curiously reminiscent of Stoic cosmology, rounded out, sometimes, also in good Stoic fashion, with a scheme of conduct. It must suffice to let W. K. Clifford (1877) speak for Moleschott (1852), Swinburne (1864), F. A. Lange and Carducci (1865), Ardigò (1877), Renan (1881), Dühring (1882), Guyau (1885), Wundt (1887), and Tolstoy (1894):[49]

"The ideal character, that which is best fitted to receive the teachings of Nature, is one which has Conscience for its motive power and Reason for its guide. The main point to be observed is that the two kinds of cosmic emotion run together and become one. The macrocosm is viewed only in relation to human action; nature is presented to the emotions as the guide and teacher of humanity. And the microcosm is viewed only as tending to complete correspondence with the external; human conduct is a subject for reverence only in so far as it is consonant to the demiurgic law, in harmony with the teaching of divine Nature. This union of the two sides of cosmic emotion belongs to the essence of the philosophic life, as the corresponding intellectual conception is of the essence of the scientific view of things." [50]

Stoicism could not well go further.

Those who had been imbued with Christianity found it an empty thing to 'love the Universe.' They feared abandonment to

"*pale despair and cold tranquillity,*
Nature's vast frame, the web of human things,
Birth and the grave, that are not as they were."

They might win to adjustment of emotion to

[168]

the structure of the universe, like George Eliot and her friend, F. W. H. Myers.[51] They might

> " *stop and say: ' There were no succor here!*
> *The aids to noble life are all within ' ! "*

finding an anodyne in Stoic acquiescence, like Matthew Arnold, and A. H. Clough.[52] Advancing from strength to strength, they might battle, and that hardly, to eternal life, like Thomas Hill Green (1884). Or they might comfort themselves with a wistful morality, attuned to the rhythm of honourable humanity, like the author of *Mark Rutherford*.[53] Be their Gethsemane or their victory what it might, Stoic impulses were very present with them all.

> " *They, winning room to see and hear,*
> *And to men's business not too near,*
> *Through clouds of individual strife*
> *Draw homeward to the general life."*

The last days are too near, and all too distracted for estimate. But, if Stoicism be recognition of the supremacy of conscience, yet " with no projections of the desired life into any juster or sterner world," its appeal cannot but continue to hold. Our contemporaries, who think themselves unfairly dealt by, harried recipients of

" The insufferable sufficiency of breath,"

will put off mordant pertness when they realize that their present clamour must recede. But, to put on high seriousness, they need to reckon with the inexorable authority of values no less than with the inexorable persistence of facts. Now, these two, and nothing but these two, set the Stoic problem. No doubt, we cannot hope to recapture Greek temperance or Roman gravity. On the other hand, we cannot escape the urge to freedom, the passion for certainty, the desire for harmony which the Stoics blazoned, if not always profoundly, at least so humanely that all might understand and, understanding, confront each his own trouble, heartened somewhat, chastened healthily.

" Inasmuch as the practical recognition of a doctrine by mankind, their acting consistently as if they believed it, is a more unequivocal proof of their belief than any expression of opinion . . . it may not be unimportant . . . that we should dwell for a little on the vast

[170]

acceptance which Stoicism experienced, and the influence which it exercised. With the single exception of Christianity . . . no form of belief ever took possession of so great a number of Europeans, or held it so long; and though it was not particularly fortunate in its expositors . . . it moulded human institutions and affected human destiny to a greater extent than all the other philosophical systems either of the ancient or modern world." [54]

I am not sure that I can accept the great jurist's every word. Enough has been said, mayhap, to indicate that he had his reasons. In any case, the irony of treating Greek and Latin as ' dead ' languages, had they given us nothing but Stoicism, may have been made plain.

NOTES AND BIBLIOGRAPHY

NOTES

1. De Quincey's forlorn excursus on " Plato's Republic,"
[in *Blackwood's Magazine*, L. (July, 1841); *Collected
Writings*, edited by D. Masson, vol. viii, pp. 42 ff., 1890],
and his exasperating essay, " Theory of Greek Tragedy "
(*ibid.*, Feb., 1840: *ibid.*, vol. x, pp. 342 ff.) may be cited
in proof. J. S. Mill's criticism, that complete non-
recognition and implied denial of a familiar principle
" are compatible with great intellectual ingenuity and
close intimacy with the subject-matter," affords the only
explanation of De Quincey's perversity (Cf. Leslie Stephen,
Hours in a Library, First Series, " De Quincey," New
York, new ed., 1904).

2. Cf. *e.g.*, Plato, *Rep.*, VII. 529.

3. The italics indicate native Athenians or those who
were so penetrated by the Athenian spirit as to be in
effect Athenians.

4. Small wonder! Although no statistics can pretend
to complete accuracy, authorities estimate that the whole
Athenian territory may have had anywhere between 310,-
000 and 425,000 inhabitants. In 431 B.C., the city of
Athens may have had a population of from 110,000
to 120,000, the free male citizens numbering from 30,000
to 44,000. In other words, striking a balance, " all Athens "
was comparable with Seattle or Cincinnati; the city
proper with New Bedford, Mass., or Trenton, N. J.; the
male free citizenry with Salem, Mass. The area of ancient Greece was almost exactly that of Lake Huron
(without Georgian Bay), comparable with New Hamp-
shire, Vermont, and Rhode Island. The area of Athenian
territory was about one fifth less than Rhode Island;
Arkansas Hot Springs Reservation or the Grand Duchy
of Luxemburg give a close approximation. It is evident,

NOTES

therefore, that the extraordinary human results demand some exercise of imagination by the modern man. Cf. A. E. Zimmern, *The Greek Commonwealth*,[3] Oxford, 1922.

5. Cf. Thucydides, II. 35 ff.

6. Cf. A. E. Zimmern, *op. cit.*

7. Cf. C. E. Robinson, *The Days of Alkibiades,* London, 1916.

8. The name Stoicism is derived from the building where Zeno and his successors met their adherents. This was the *Stoa Pœcile* (Painted Porch). Originally called the Peisianaction, because erected by Peisianax (uncle of Alcibiades, son-in-law of Cimon), it must have been built *c.* 460–50 B.C. It consisted of a long colonnade, with an open court (peristyle) in the rear. Seats were provided where men might lounge. The building was spacious enough to be used sometimes for public purposes; for example, as the criminal court under the government of the Thirty (Critias, Theramenes, 404 B.C.). Æschines refers to it as one of the loveliest things in the Agora (Meeting Place, Market Place). Paintings by the great artists Polygnotus (a close friend of Cimon) and Micon enriched it. " Theseus and the Athenians fighting the Amazons . . . the scene when the Greeks have captured Ilium . . . the combatants at Marathon . . . of the warriors the most conspicuous in the painting are Callimachus, Miltiades, Echetlus," as Pausanias records. The Porch has disappeared entirely, indeed its site is matter of conjecture. We know that it was situated in the Ceramicus, or Potters' Ward, of Athens. The likelihood is that it stood on the northwest corner of the " Meeting Place," to the left entering by the Dipylon Gate, perhaps almost on the site of the extant remains of the Stoa of the Giants. Cf. Charles Heald Weller, *Athens and its Monuments,* pp. 123 ff., New York, 1913.

9. Cf. W. W. Tarn, *Antigonos Gonatas,* Oxford, 1913.

10. Cf. F. Cumont, *The Oriental Religions in Roman Paganism,* p. 164, Chicago, 1911.

11. Cf. *Quaestiones Tusc.,* II. 22.

NOTES

12. The drift toward cults which would or could offer
personal, *private* comfort over and above ceremonial participation in the State religion, had begun before Cicero's
time. His books bear definite witness to this yearning
for assurance, in short, to the cry for faith. The following incidents, a few selected from many, may serve to
indicate earlier symptoms of infiltration by ' oriental '
religions into the Italian area; to suggest how unstable
and transitional was the age in which Cicero became the
great intellectual, Julius Cæsar, the great political mediator
between their own and the later epoch. One need but
associate significant movements with the events or names.
All dates are B.C. Rites of the Great Mother of Ida in
Rome (204). Probable date of the completion of the
translation of the Hebrew Scriptures into Greek (the
Septuagint) for the benefit of the Greek-speaking Jews of
the Diaspora (150). " Chaldæans " (*i.e.* astrologers) ban-
ished from Rome (139), indicating opposition to a movement which Posidonius made respectable. The Sicilian
Servile War led by a Syrian slave, a votary of Atargatis
(134). Death of Carneades; spread of scepticism about
man's ability to solve religious and metaphysical questions
by rational methods (129). Serapis becomes a prominent
deity under the Ptolemies in Egypt; a Serapeium at
Pozzuoli in Campania (104). Posidonius travels in the
west (100). Roman soldiers learn to worship Mâ the
chief goddess of the two Comanas, during the Mithridatic
wars (88–81); Sulla introduced her rites into Rome.
Antiochus lectures at Athens, softening scepticism (78);
Cicero resorts to him. Sulla participates in the Mysteries of Mithra (67). Cicero, Consul (63). Official (senatorial) appeal to the Sibylline Books in the matter of
the restoration to Cicero of his home on the Palatine
(57). Death of Lucretius, the great spokesman of Epicurean materialism (55). Death of Cato, the ensample of
Stoic sobriety and devotion (46). Murder of Julius
Cæsar by republicans whom Stoicism affected profoundly
(44). Battle of Actium (31). Death of Varro, second
only to Cicero as an intellectual power (28). The cru-

cial date is probably the transportation of the Magna Mater fetish to the Palatine (April, 204).

13. Cf. *Ann.* XIII. 3.

14. Samuel Dill, *Roman Society from Nero to Marcus Aurelius,* p. 295, London, 1905. It is not too much to say that this admirable work is *the* guide to the complex period with which it deals.

15. Cf. Richard Mott Gummere, *Seneca the Philosopher and his Modern Message* (in this *Series*).

16. Cf. the utilitarian cant and superficial history of philosophy in the essay, " Lord Bacon."

17. Epictetus, *Diss.,* III. xii. The whole chapter is important as giving Epictetus' ideal.

18. Cf. *ibid.,* II. xix.

19. Cf. *Instit. Or.,* I. Prooem., 10–19: X. 1, 35, 123–31: XI. 1, 33–35; 3, 12: XII. 2, 4–9, 25–26.

20. Cf. Cardinal John Henry Newman, *The Idea of a University.*[6] pp. 194 ff., London, 1886.

21. Reuben Shapcott (*pseud.* for William Hale White), *Mark Rutherford's Deliverance,* pp. 207, 210, London, 1885.

22. Grant that there must be a Nature (*phusis*) or " world-stuff," persistent by comparison with all passing shapes, because uncreated and indestructible; then all things are its phases. As a self-evident matter of course, not only motion (the Atomists' view), but also life, sensation, and reason inhere in it. This is Hylozoism as the Greeks conceived it. It is not a doctrine concerned to eliminate the real existence of life and thought after the manner of modern Hylozoism (*e.g.,* Diderot and Buffon). Identify Zeus (god) with the world envisaged in this way, and you have Stoic Pantheism. Hence the " World-soul," not as a Demiurge (a created fabricator of the world), but as the efficient cause of perception and reason (in addition to orderly motion and sequence) in the universe as a whole.

23. Sara Teasdale in *American Poetry,* pp. 100, 91, New York, 1922.

24. First published in *Ideals of Science and the Faith,*

NOTES

Essays by Various Authors, edited by the Rev. J. E. Hand, pp. 157 ff., London and New York, 1904; reprinted in *Mysticism and Logic,*[2] pp. 46 ff., London, 1919.

25. J. B. Lightfoot, D.D., *St. Paul's Epistle to the Philippians,*[3] p. 301, London, 1873.

26. *Ibid.,* p. 293.

27. T. R. Glover, *Progress in Religion,* pp. 294-5, London, 1922. Cf. P. Gardner, *Evolution in Christian Ethics,* London, 1919.

28. Cf. E. de Faye, *Clément d'Alexandrie,* Paris, 1898.

29. Cf. R. Thamin, *Saint Ambrose et la morale chrétienne au IV*e* siècle,* Paris, 1895; P. Pourrat, *Christian Spirituality,* New York, 1922.

30. Cf. Henry Osborn Taylor, *The Classical Heritage of the Middle Ages,*[2] New York, 1903; has a useful bibliography.

31. Cf. Paul Lehmann, *Die Parodie im Mittelalter,* Munich, 1922. Note Hildebert's eclectic Stoicism in his lines *Ad Patrem,* the first part of an *Oratio devotissima ad tres personas sanctissimae Trinitatis,* beginning, *Super cuncta, subter cuncta,* which seem to foreshadow St. Thomas Aquinas' body-soul formula — *Tota in toto et tota in aliqua parte.* Hildebert also wrote *A Little Treatise on the Four Virtues of a Good Life,* obviously indebted to Cicero, and therefore to Stoic moralism; while such lines as *Quae summa boni est? Mens conscia recti,* reproduce Stoic phrases. Cf. Migne, *Pat. Lat.,* vol. 171, cols. 1411, 1438.

32. W. E. H. Lecky, *History of European Morals,* vol. ii, p. 45, London, 1869.

33. Cf. Henry Osborn Taylor, *Thought and Expression in the Sixteenth Century,* 2 vols., New York, 1920.

34. Cf. Walter C. Summers, *Select Letters of Seneca,* Introdn., pp. xcvi ff., London, 1910.

35. Cf. A. H. Douglas, *The Philosophy and Psychology of Pietro Pomponazzi,* Cambridge, England, 1910; C. C. J. Webb, *Studies in the History of Natural Theology,* pp. 323 ff., Oxford, 1915.

36. Cf. Léontine Zanta, *La Renaissance du Stoicisme au*

XVIe siècle, Paris, 1914; Basil Anderton, Sketches from a *Library Window,* pp. 1–30, Cambridge, England, 1922. Zanta illustrates the overstress mentioned on p. 140.

37. Published in 1690, eight years after the author's death.

38. Cf. T. M. Lindsay, *A History of the Reformation,* 2 vols., New York, 1906–7; Preserved Smith, *The Age of the Reformation,* New York, 1920.

39. J. A. Leighton, *The Field of Philosophy,* p. 149, definitive edn., New York, 1923.

40. Cf. R. W. and A. J. Carlyle, *A History of Mediæval Political Theory in the West,* 4 vols. so far; vols. i–iii are referred to here, Edinburgh and London, 1903–22.

41. Cf. *Religion innerhalb der Grenzen der bloss. Vernunft,* Bk. ii. sect. 3

42. Cf. J. N. Figgis, *From Gerson to Grotius,* Cambridge, England, 1907; O. Gierke, *Political Theories of the Middle Age, translated with an Introduction* by F. W. Maitland, *ibid.,* 1900; more fully, in his *Das deutsche Genossenschaftsrecht,* vol. iii, Berlin, 1881; of which Maitland translates sect 11. For Gierke's interpretation of Natural Right, cf. vol. iv, sects. 14–17, *ibid.* 1913.

43. Cf. J. N. Figgis, *The Divine Right of Kings,*[2] Cambridge, England, 1914.

44. Cf. *Essays Moral, Political, and Literary,* edited by T. H. Green and T. H. Grose, vol. i, pp. 203 ff., London, 1875.

45. Cf. James Orr on " J. S. Mill and Christianity," in *The Theological Monthly,* VI. 8 ff., 108 ff. (1891).

46. 1821–1881. The extraordinary impression made by the *Journal Intime* indicates that it expressed a common mood of the time. The English-speaking world could scarce produce an Amiel; Mark Pattison is the nearest parallel. Echoes — if there be an *original* echo — might be found in *The Education of Henry Adams.* Cf. *Amiel's Journal, translated with an Introduction and Notes,* by Mrs. Humphry Ward, London, 1890; *Memoirs,* by Mark Pattison, London, 1885.

47. Kleist, Platen, Lenau, and Rückert among the poets;

NOTES

Schleiermacher, C. A. Nitzsch, Daub, Marheineke, D. F. Strauss, Khanis, Hundeshagen, C. C. J. von Bunsen, Hase, L. I. Rückert, Schenkel, and Biedermann among the theologians, are examples.

48. *Sartor Resartus,* Bk. iii, chapter viii *ad fin.*

49. The dates appended to the names indicate the publication of a work in which the tendencies under discussion may be traced; *e.g.,* Tolstoy's *Christianity and Patriotism,* Moscow, 1894; in vol. XX of *Complete Works,* London and New York, 1905.

50. *Lectures and Essays, with an Introduction by F. Pollock,*[2] p. 405, London and New York, 1886.

51. *Fragments of Prose and Poetry, edited by Eveleen Myers,* pp. 17 ff., London and New York, 1904.

52. Cf. Walter Bagehot, *Literary Studies,* vol. ii, p. 299 ff., London, 1879.

53. William Hale White (1831–1913). *The Autobiography of Mark Rutherford, Dissenting Minister,* London, 1881; *Mark Rutherford's Deliverance* (1885); *The Revolution in Tanner's Lane* (1887); *The Early Life of Mark Rutherford* (1913). As I write, Messrs. T. Fisher Unwin announce a complete edition (six volumes) with some account of the author. To be published in the United States by the G. H. Doran Company, New York.

54. James Lorimer, *The Institutes of Law, a Treatise of the Principles of Jurisprudence as Determined by Nature,*[2] pp. 150, 151, Edinburgh and London, 1880.

[181]

BIBLIOGRAPHY

I. The general reader will be well served by Dill and Zimmern (see Notes 4 and 14 above), and by the following:

HICKS, R. D., *Stoic and Epicurean,* in the Series "Epochs of Philosophy." New York, 1910. Has an illuminating "Chronological Table," and a "Select Bibliography" in which special attention should be paid to "Indispensable Collections of Material."

RENDALL, G. H., *Marcus Aurelius Antoninus to Himself: an English Translation with Introductory Study on Stoicism and the Last of the Stoics.* London and New York, 1896. Within its compass, the "Introductory Study" is the best account of Stoicism in English.

SEDGWICK, H. D., *Marcus Aurelius, a Biography told as much as may be by Letters, together with some Account of the Stoic Religion and an Exposition of the Roman Government's Attempt to suppress Christianity during Marcus's Reign.* New Haven, 1921. The Bibliography and Appendix D are specially valuable in connection with the ancient authorities, some of which may be obtained most conveniently in "The Loeb Classical Library." New York and London.

PATER, WALTER, *Marius the Epicurean, his Sensations and Ideas.* 2 vols. London, 1885. Reprinted in "The Modern Library." New York, 1920.

TAYLOR, H., *Cicero, a Sketch of his Life and Works: a Commentary on the Roman Constitution and Roman Public Life, supplemented by the Sayings of Cicero*

[182]

arranged for the first time as an Anthology. Chicago, 1916.

ZELLER, E., *The Stoics, Epicureans and Sceptics,* translation by Oswald J. Reichel. London, 1880. This is still the great storehouse of learning in detail.

II. A model bibliography of Stoicism (till 1910) is given by Professor E. Vernon Arnold in *Roman Stoicism,* pp. 437 ff. Cambridge, England, 1911. On p. 438 (line 20 from foot) substitute Bussell, F. W. for *Russell, E..W.* Some later works are:

ADAM, J., *The Vitality of Platonism.* Cambridge, England, 1911.

ADAMSON, R., *The Development of Greek Philosophy.* Edinburgh and London, 1908.

APELT, O., *Diogenes Laertius. Leben u. Meinungen berühmter Philosophen.* 2 Bde. Leipzig, 1921.

BARKER, E., *Greek Political Theory.* Vol. I. " Plato and his Predecessors." New edition, London, 1918.

BARTH, H., *Die Seele in d. Philosophie Platons.* Tübingen, 1921.

BARTH, P., *Die Stoa.*⁴ Stuttgart, 1922.

BEVAN, E., *Stoics and Sceptics.* Oxford, 1913.

BIGNONE, E., *Epicuro.* Bari, 1920.

BISSING, F. W. VON, *Griechentum u. seine Weltmission.* Leipzig, 1920.

BONHÖFFER, A., *Epiktet u. d. Neue Testament.* Giessen, 1911.

BRÉHIER, É., *Chrysippe.* Paris, 1910.

BROCHARD, V., *Études de Philosophie Ancienne et de Philosophie Moderne.* Paris, 1912.

BROCK, M. D., *Studies in Fronto and his Age.* Cambridge, England, 1911.

CASE, S., *The Evolution of Early Christianity: a Genetic Study of first-century Christianity in relation to its Religious Environment.* Chicago, 1914.

BIBLIOGRAPHY

CORNIL, G., *Droit Romain*. Brussels, 1921.

D'ALTON, J. F., *Horace and his Age: a Study in Historical Background*. London, 1917.

DIELS, H., *Der antike Pessimismus*. Berlin, 1921.

DRACHMANN, A. B., *Atheism in Pagan Antiquity*. London and Copenhagen, 1922.

FOWLER, W. W., *The Religious Experience of the Roman People*. London and New York, 1911. *Roman Ideas of Deity in the last Century before the Christian Era*. Ibid. 1914. *Roman Essays and Interpretations*. Oxford, 1920.

FRANK, T., *Vergil, a Biography*. Oxford, 1922.

GERHÄUSSER, W., *Der Protreptikos d. Poseidonios*. Munich, 1912.

GILBERT, O., *Griechische Religionsphilosophie*. Leipzig, 1911.

GOMPERZ, H., *Die Lebensauffassung d. griechischen Philosophen u. d. Ideal d. inneren Freiheit.*[2] Leipzig, 1915.

GORDON, G. S. (ed.), " Ciceronianism " by A. C. Clark, in *English Literature and the Classics*. Oxford, 1912.

HARNACK, A. VON, *Marcion*. Leipzig, 1921.

HEINEMANN, J., *Poseidonios' metaphysische Schriften*. I Bd. Dresden, 1921.

HEITLAND, W. E., *The Roman Fate*. Cambridge, England, 1922.

HOLLAND, F., *Seneca*. London, 1920.

HUIT, C., *Les Origines Grecques du Stoicisme*. Paris, 1900.

JAEGER, W. W., *Nemesios von Emesa. Quellenforschungen z. Neuplatonismus u. s. Anfänge bei Poseidonios*. Berlin, 1914.

JOËL. K., *Geschichte d. antiken Philosophie*. I Bd. Tübingen, 1921.

KAERST, J., *Geschichte d. Hellenismus.*[2] I Bd. Leipzig, 1917.

LABRIOLLE, P. DE, *Histoire de la Littérature Latine Chrétienne*. Paris, 1921.

LITCHFIELD, H. W., " National *Exempla Virtutis* in Roman

Literature," in *Harvard Studies in Classical Philology*, xxv. 1–71 (1914).

LIVINGSTONE, R. W. (ed.), "Philosophy" by J. Burnet; "Political Thought" by A. E. Zimmern; "Religion" by W. R. Inge in *The Legacy of Greece*. Oxford, 1922.

LUCAS, F. L., *Seneca and Elizabethan Tragedy*. Chapter II. "Seneca the Man." Cambridge, England, 1922.

MACCHIORO, V., *Eraclito*. Bari, 1922.

MATHESON, P. E., *Epictetus. The Discourses and Manual*, Translation. 2 vols. Oxford, 1915.

MIELI, A., *Storia Generale del Pensiero Scientifico*. Vol. I., "La Scuola Ionica. La Scuola Pythagorica. La Scuola Eleata; Heracleitus." Florence, 1916.

MOORE, C. H., *The Religious Thought of the Greeks from Homer to the Triumph of Christianity*. Cambridge, Massachusetts, 1916.

MORE, P. E., *Hellenistic Philosophies*. Princeton, New Jersey, 1923.

MURRAY, G., *Essays and Addresses*. London, 1921; published as *Tradition and Progress*. Boston, 1922.

NORDEN, E., *Der Agnostos Theos u. s. w.* Leipzig u. Berlin, 1913. *Die germanische Urgeschichte in Tacitus' Germania*. Leipzig, 1920.

PETERSSON, T., *Cicero, a Biography*. Berkeley, California, 1920.

PÖHLMAN, R. VON, *Die Weltanschauung d. Tacitus*, Munich, 1913. *Cf*. Fabia, P., in *Journal des Savants*, xiii. 250 ff. (1914).

PRELLER, H., *Das Altertum, seine staatliche u. geistliche Entwicklung u. deren Nachwirkung*. Leipzig, 1920.

REINHARDT, K., *Poseidonios*. Munich, 1921.

REITZENSTEIN, R., *Die hellenistischen Mysterienreligionen.*[2] Leipzig u. Berlin, 1922.

RITCHIE, D. G., *Natural Rights: a Criticism of some Political and Ethical Conceptions*. London and New York, 1895.

ROBIN, L., *Études sur la Signification et la Place de la Physique dans la Philosophie de Platon*. Paris, 1919.

BIBLIOGRAPHY

ROSTAGNI, A., *Giuliano l'Apostata*. Turin, 1920.

RUDBERG, G., *Forschungen zu Poseidonios*. Upsala, 1918.

SABIN, E., *Platon u. d. griechischen Utopie*. Munich, 1921.

SANDYS, J. E. (ed.), " Roman Philosophy " by R. D. Hicks, in *Companion to Latin Studies*. Cambridge, England, 1910.

SEECK, O., *Geschichte d. Untergangs d. antiken Welt*. 6 Bde. Berlin, 1895–1920.

SHARP, D. S., *Epictetus and the New Testament*. London, 1914.

SIEBECK, H., *Die Umbildung d. peripatetischen Naturphilosophie in die der Stoiker.*[2] Freiburg i. B., 1888.

SIHLER, E. G., *Cicero of Arpinum*. New Haven, 1914.

SONNENSCHEIN, E. A., " Stoicism in English Literature," in *The Contemporary Review*, cxxiv. 355 ff. (1923).

Teubner Texts, the most recent: *e.g.*, Hense's and Hosius's Seneca; Plasberg's (*de N.D.*), Pohlenz's (*Tusc. Dis.*), Schiche's (*de Fin.*) Cicero; Schenkl's M. Aurelius.

TOURTOULAN, P., *Philosophy in the Development of Law*. New York, 1922.

WALTZ, R., *Vie de Sénèque*. Paris, 1909.

WENDLAND, P., *Die hellenistisch-römische Kultur in ihren Beziehungen z. Judentum u. Christentum.*[3] Tübingen, 1912.

WESTAWAY, F. W., *The Educational Theory of Plutarch*. London, 1922.

WUNDT, M., *Geschichte d. griechische Ethik*. 2 Bde. Bd. II., " Der Hellenismus." Leipzig, 1908–11.

ZANTA, L., *La Traduction Française du Manuel d'Épictète d'André de Rivaudeau*. Paris, 1914.

ZELLER, E., *Die Philosophie d. Griechen u. s. w.* Hrsg. von W. Nestle. VI Ausg. in progress. I T., I u. II Hälfte. Leipzig, 1919–20.

ZIELINSKI, TH., *Cicero im Wandel d. Jahrhunderte.*[3] Leipzig u. Berlin, 1912.

INDEX

INDEX

INDEX

INDEX

Marcus Aurelius Antoninus, 4, 26, 61, 68 f, 85, 105 f, 113 f, 118, 122
Marsilius of Padua, 152
Martianus Capella, 127
Mary, Queen of Scots, 155
Maximus of Tyre, 62, 115
Megarians, 17, 76
Mela, 57
Melancthon, 153
Meynell, Mrs., 109
Middleton, Conyers, 155
Mill, J. S., 162, 175
Milton, 128
Minucius Felix, 125
Moleschott, 167
Mommsen, 155
Monasticism, 123
Montaigne, 142, 156
Montanism, 123, 126
Myers, F. W. H., 169, 181
Myth, viii

Napoleon, 162
Natural Religion, 119, 157 f
Nature, viii, 104 f
Nature, Law of, 131 f, 137, 158
Neoplatonism, 117, 133, 147
Neopythagoreanism, 126, 134
Neo-Stoicism, vi, 134, 167 f
Nero, 52, 61, 67
Nerva, 53, 73
Newton, 155
Nicolas of Cusa, 143
Nigidius Figulus, Publius, 113
Nietzsche, 123

Occam, 136
Old Academy, 17
One and Many, 79 f
Ovid, 136

Pagan Reaction, the, 38 f, 89 f, 177 f
Painted Porch, the, 176
Panaetius, 21 f
Pascal, 153, 154
Pattison, Mark, 147, 180
Paul, St., 57, 89, 114, 115 f, 123 f, 152
Pelagius, 153, 165
Pericles, 3, 5 f, 10, 50
Persius, 51, 136, 155
Peter of Blois, 135
Peter Damianus, 135
Phidias, 3
Philo, 26, 89, 119
Plato, v, viii, 3, 5, 13, 14, 22, 74, 76, 80, 94, 117, 133, 151, 159
Pliny the Elder, 56, 91
Pliny the Younger, 91
Plotinus, 25
Plutarch, 62, 67, 116
Polemo, 13
Polybius, 33
Polygnotus, 3, 176
Pomponazzi, 143, 144 f, 179
Porphyry, 135
Posidonius, 21, 24, 36, 43, 74, 90, 150
Praxiteles, 3
Prodicus, 3, 7
Protagoras, 3, 7
Protestantism, 128, 148 f, 165

[192]

INDEX

Providence, 105
Pyrrhus, 11

Rabelais, 142
Rationalism, 156
Renan, 108, 167
Rhetoric, 23 f, 37, 57
Roman civilization, corruption of, 41 f
Romanticism, 163 f
Roman Stoicism, 25 f, 38 f, 99 f, 118 f, 128 f, 141, 143, 150, 151, 155
Rudolph Agricola, 141
Rufinus, 150
Ruskin, 165
Russell, Bertrand, 108, 178 f

Salamis, 6
Schiller, 164
Schools, Greek philosophical, 12 f
Schopenhauer, 39
Schoppe, Caspar, 147
Scipio, 27
Senate, the Roman, 28 f, 36, 47 f
Seneca, 26, 38, 46, 55 f, 90, 93, 102, 113, 114, 118, 133, 134, 136, 141, 143, 147, 150, 153, 157, 162
Shaftesbury, 158
Shelley, 161, 165
Simplicius, 72
Smith, Adam, 161
Socrates, v, 3, 4, 7, 13, 35, 64, 76, 94, 125, 163
Sophists, 8 f
Sophocles, 3

Spinoza, 50, 155, 156
Stephen, L., 175
Stilpo, 13
Stoa Poecile, 176
Stoic ' accommodation,' 90 f
Stoic cosmopolitanism, 11 f, 118 f
Stoic dogmas, 74 f
Stoic epistemology, 86 f
Stoic ethics, 87 f, 96 f, 160 f
Stoic hylozoism, 82 f, 146, 178
Stoic martyrs, 53 f
Stoic Monism, 86, 159 f
Stoic ' opposition ' at Rome, 44 f, 154
Stoic Philosophy, scope of 77 f
Stoic Rationalism, 118 f
Stoicism, Early, 14 f
Stoicism, influence of, 170 f
Stoicism and Latin Christianity, 132 f
Stoicism, Middle, 21 f
Stoicism in Modern Thought, 159 f
Stoicism and the ' Preparation for Christianity,' 121 f
Stoicism and Semitism, 15 f
Stoicism and the Renaissance, 139 f, 154 f
Stoicism and the Reformation, 149 f, 154 f
Stoicism, Roman, 25 f, 38 f, 99 f, 118 f, 128 f, 141, 143, 150, 151, 155
Stoicism and Roman Law, 128 f, 137 f

INDEX

Our Debt to Greece and Rome

AUTHORS AND TITLES

AUTHORS AND TITLES

AESCHYLUS AND SOPHOCLES. *J. T. Sheppard.*

GREEK RELIGION. *Walter Woodburn Hyde.*

SURVIVALS OF ROMAN RELIGION. *Gordon J. Laing.*

MYTHOLOGY. *Jane Ellen Harrison.*

ANCIENT BELIEFS IN THE IMMORTALITY OF THE SOUL. *Clifford H. Moore.*

STAGE ANTIQUITIES. *James Turney Allen.*

PLAUTUS AND TERENCE. *Gilbert Norwood.*

ROMAN POLITICS. *Frank Frost Abbott.*

PSYCHOLOGY, ANCIENT AND MODERN. *G. S. Brett.*

ANCIENT AND MODERN ROME. *Rodolfo Lanciani.*

WARFARE BY LAND AND SEA. *Eugene S. McCartney.*

THE GREEK FATHERS. *James Marshall Campbell.*

GREEK BIOLOGY AND MEDICINE. *Henry Osborn Taylor.*

MATHEMATICS. *David Eugene Smith.*

LOVE OF NATURE AMONG THE GREEKS AND ROMANS. *H. R. Fairclough.*

ANCIENT WRITING AND ITS INFLUENCE. *B. L. Ullman.*

GREEK ART. *Arthur Fairbanks.*

ARCHITECTURE. *Alfred M. Brooks.*

ENGINEERING. *Alexander P. Gest.*

MODERN TRAITS IN OLD GREEK LIFE. *Charles Burton Gulick.*

ROMAN PRIVATE LIFE. *Walton Brooks McDaniel.*

GREEK AND ROMAN FOLKLORE. *William Reginald Halliday.*

ANCIENT EDUCATION. *J. F. Dobson.*